11/77

aberrational

Appalachia's Children

David H. Looff

Appalachia's Children

The Challenge of
Mental Health

The University
Press of Kentucky

Standard Book Number: 8131–1241–9

Library of Congress Catalog Card Number: 78–132830

Copyright © 1971 by The University Press of Kentucky

A statewide cooperative scholarly publishing agency
serving Berea College, Centre College of Kentucky,
Eastern Kentucky University, Kentucky State College,
Morehead State University, Murray State University,
University of Kentucky, University of Louisville,
and Western Kentucky University.

Editorial and Sales Offices: Lexington, Kentucky 40506

To Roger, Joanne, Ralph, Betty Sue . . .
and the other children of Eastern Kentucky

Now I am old my teachers are the young.
What can't be molded must be cracked and sprung.
I strain at lessons fit to start a suture.
I go to school to youth to learn the future.
—Robert Frost

Contents

Foreword

There is always an excitement when one encounters a breakthrough. This is particularly true when it opens new solutions to an old, resistant and painful problem. That is the feeling with which I read Dr. Looff's manuscript for this book. The problem is Appalachia.

Appalachia has been a thorn in the side of the United States for more than a hundred years. While Negro slaves were being set free, another type of slavery was evolving in the rough Appalachian mountains, locked in by geography and bypassed by a rapidly developing country and economy, until, as Jack Weller describes it in *Yesterday's People,* Appalachia became synonymous with destitution and backwardness.

Appalachia, however, represents a different version of the cycle of poverty from that seen in the ghettos of our inner cities. Dr. Looff highlights from his studies processes that are determinants of the developmental experiences and resulting personality patterns which, from generation to generation, lock in the inner forces and perpetuate self-defeating attitudes. These, combined with the problems of economics and geography, provide the basis for the resistance to change which has marked the attempts at intervention to modify the attitudes and life-style of the mountain people. This developmental process ends with what has been described as "the pride and privatism of people unable to compete outside the ancient kinships of the hollow."

What is so impressive and yet disheartening is the evidence we have from this report about how early the process begins in the life cycle. ·The problems begin long before children reach school age. It is not only the schools therefore which account for the highest school dropout rates in the country and one of the highest illiteracy rates (Appalachia is reported to lose 90,000 high school students each year).

The Joint Commission on the Mental Health of Children in its recently completed studies emphasized that one cannot separate health from mental health and that both of these cannot be separated from social and cultural forces. It is noteworthy that Dr. Looff approached his studies by working on a multidisciplinary basis, through and with public health nurses and social workers, while maintaining ties with the schools. Also he worked at the individual family level instead of in the usual programmatic approaches in which there are "trickle-down" effects from inputs at the top level of the mountain communities. Is there not a lesson here for those with responsibility for reaching the roots of the problem of Appalachia?

The Committee on Children of Minority Groups of the Joint Commission on the Mental Health of Children considers the children of Appalachia as part of a discriminated-against minority in the United States. The problem of racism is not confined to the black-, yellow-, or red-skinned child. The resulting image the child develops as part of a group that is looked down on from the outside can be self-defeating. This committee's report states:

The mainstream culture has yet to learn from its history that people can rise out of poverty to become contributing members of society only to plunge again into the depths of want and dependency when society withdraws the means for self-sufficiency. Appalachia has taught us nothing. The once independent mountaineer family is slowly disintegrating; its fate is now linked to those forces which determine the stability of the oppressed nonwhite. It, too, is falling victim to lack of economic opportunity plus a welfare system which perpetuates poverty and lowers self-esteem. The mainstream culture barricades itself against the weakness of its cultural and socio-economic system by formulating racist rationalizations. Individuals— and even races—are held responsible for their own plight; inequality of opportunity is ignored. After generations of isolation and poverty, the oppressed themselves begin to doubt their own self-worth; a "self-fulfilling prophecy" arises from these doubts—one easily reinforced by the rationalizations and inequalities perpetuated by the majority.

Dr. Looff's studies have their foundations in our basic information about personality development. They report on the fundamental components which determine what kind of individual emerges from the earliest relationship experiences. They begin with patterns of dependency and follow these through to the influence of the infant's and young child's dependency experience on his development of trust or lack of it. When the child begins to experiment before the end of the first year with independence and separation, fears emerge; Dr. Looff examines them in terms of how they can mold the child into fearfulness of the outside world. The events which cause the child to lose faith in his body are traced into the influence they have on physical symptoms, which in turn can be incapacitating and establish poor self-confidence. Then there is noted in the next developmental steps how the interweaving of dependency, separation, and poor body-image with inborn impulses, aggressive and sexual, can further complicate the patterns of functioning. It is in this area that cultural patterns offer only partial solutions to mastery over these impulses, particularly if constructive and creative directions for their investment such as learning are not available. When one combines all these deficits in personality development with the necessary emphasis on the struggle for survival which the isolated family faces, a picture emerges of the bareness that is the condition of mountain life. The basic ingredients are then present which provide distortion of the golden rule, "Do unto others [your children] as others have done unto you."

More than seven billion dollars of public funds have been poured into the Appalachian area in the last ten years. It is estimated that a million of the poor in the region have not been reached in spite of what has been described as "an extraordinary effort—a policy of favoritism to overcome prior-neglect unmatched in American History." It becomes obvious that, once distorted personal and living patterns are laid down in the individuals for whom the programs are established, job opportunities, training or retraining programs, bringing in new roads and industry are too late for those who are "locked in."

It all seems to add up to looking back to where the problems begin. This is what *Appalachia's Children* does. When we look at the information which Dr. Looff makes available in his book we can see new hope for solving the tough problem that Appalachia has been to the forces brought to bear to assimilate its inhabitants and bring them into the mainstream of American life. The implication of this work is that we must start at the beginning of the problems, with the very young children. The Appalachian Regional Commission has recently made available a set of reports titled "Programs for Infants and Young Children." If one combines such approaches with the information from this book, there is a blueprint available for reaching the problems of Appalachia where they start, in the fundamental patterns which close-in the individual and make it difficult for many to accept change. The children of Appalachia are born with potentials which are too often never realized. Let us try to see to it that they develop into individuals who can make choices and accept change.

The process of development we are talking about does not take place overnight or even in a few years. The implications of this book are that we can have hope for Appalachia, but we must also have patience—and multidisciplinary diligence.

Reginald S. Lourie, M.D.

Preface

This is a book about the children of Eastern Kentucky. By extrapolation, it is also a book about the children of the Southern Appalachian region, of which Eastern Kentucky is an integral part, and it may in the end reflect on the lives of children all across that wider region we call the rural South. What I attempt to do here is to organize and draw conclusions from the impressions I have gained as a clinical child psychiatrist engaged in fieldwork in Eastern Kentucky over a six-year period, impressions both of child development in the area and of the results of that development—the mental health or mental disorder of the children themselves. Thus I present my perceptions of the ways in which present-day Eastern Kentucky families raise their children and my clinical conclusions concerning the kinds of adjustments to life that these children make.

The children described in this book are in a real sense not "all children." Since no child grows up in a vacuum, the children of Eastern Kentucky cannot be understood apart from the historical, geographic, and socioeconomic characteristics of the area in which they grow. Knowledge of the children requires some knowledge of the lives of parents, teachers, and the many others upon whom they are dependent. Moreover, the behavior of any person over his life-span is more complex than any of us can imagine. Given this as fact, the best I feel I can do is to muster confidence that developmental order is to be found here; that from the facts we gather we can discern relevant forces and factors that enable us to compare the early and later life relationships of these children. Here our own clinical work in child development and mental health in Eastern Kentucky complements what has been observed in the past about the structure and functioning of Southern Appalachian family life and about forces in the development of the region itself. Our work and this book represent, therefore, an attempt to extend what is already known about this particular people and their region into the area of their children's mental health.

Eastern Kentucky has long been considered one of the most dramatic examples of a depressed region. Distress of all kinds is severe and long-lasting. Unemployment, underemployment, disease, out-migration of many people in the potential labor force who leave behind their old kin and the children, low educational levels, lack of any economic balance, marginal agriculture—all these problems remain both chronic and acute. They cry out for solutions that thus far either have evaded the efforts of local groups and federal and state programs or at best have made progress at a pace graphically described by one Eastern Kentuckian as "slow whittling." It is against such a socioeconomic backdrop that this clinical book is cast.

I say "clinical" because it is our actual experiences in field clinics that provide whatever is new and of special value about the book. Our relationships with children and their families were the heart of these experiences, and they are in turn the heart of the book. Everything else here exists either as an aid to understanding the clinical experiences, as a background for them, or as a conclusion drawn from them.

One of my own biases as a child psychiatrist will be clear throughout, namely, that I, along with many others, view mental disorders as social phenomena much more than as objective, constitutionally given conditions of individual persons. Mental disorder—or mental health—is firmly embedded in a social matrix.

Our activities in Eastern Kentucky have all been made possible by what we call the Manchester Project. Over a six-year period (1964-1970) the project furnished the clinical observations that are detailed here. As our work in the project's psychiatric field clinics proceeded, we found that we were gathering a great deal of data about what seemed at first to be quite different, or discrete, syndromes or clusters of mental disorders in the children. But we later came to view them as similar beads on a single developmental thread; to understand each cluster as being more kin to than separate from the others, and the entire group of entities as being outgrowths of the unique developmental themes of the region in which the children were growing up. At this point it seems crucial to indicate that our clinical studies did not represent epidemiological data on all mental disorders of all the children in the area served by the project during the six-year period. I should also say that there are other biases—those arising from our individual background interests and kinds of training as psychiatrists and social workers—which affected how we as clinicians selected certain data as we met with the many children and their families over the years. Therefore, the generalizations I draw from our large clinical sample to what other families and children are like are to some extent biased.

I discuss also the way in which the seemingly discrete clinical clusters are related and attempt to synthesize our observations by drawing a correlation between the developmental forces shaping the children and our clinical observations of what becomes of them in terms of mental health and mental disorder.

The chapters in the section called "New Paths" represent an effort to extend what we learned clinically about the children of Eastern Kentucky into suggestions for redirecting certain aspects or areas of their development, although this book is not primarily concerned with planning or policy. It is really a clinical report. The part called "Backgrounds" will, I hope, serve the same function for the reader as it served for our clinical team. We started our work by reviewing that of others, so that we were firmly in context. The essence of that review, as well as of background work of our own, is included here.

Let there be at the outset no misunderstanding on one point: I profoundly respect the inherently strong family structure and ties of those from this region who have shared themselves and their children with us. Although I detail instances of mental disorder in the children, and instances of failure in family functioning, I would be wrong if I did not underscore at the same time family strengths or did not sharply define them as sources of hope.

Overall, in this book I try to demonstrate the profound need for increased concern about what is happening to the rising generation—the children of Eastern Kentucky, the children of the Southern Appalachian region, and the children of the rural South. What kinds of persons are developing here, capable of realizing what future opportunities in their local or national setting? It is on this question, above all, that our clinical observations focus our attention.

The work on which this book is based was initiated and financed as a joint clinical service-teaching-research project by the Department of Psychiatry of the University of Kentucky College of Medicine and the local health departments of Clay, Jackson, Lee, and Owsley counties in Eastern Kentucky. Shortly after it began, the Manchester Project, as the work came to be called, received a continuing-education grant from the National Institutes of Mental Health. Having given their commitment to this work, the professional staffs of these agencies are thus among those who are rightfully included in my acknowledgments. From the outset, Joseph B. Parker, Jr., M.D., former professor and chairman of the Department of Psychiatry, and Mildred B. Gabbard, M.D., health officer of the four counties in which the work was located, were close collaborators. As professional colleagues, they gave unstintingly of themselves and their time in every phase of the planning and the operation of the Manchester Project.

This work has depended upon the cooperation and support of literally hundreds of people. No acknowledgments can adequately express my appreciation of their help, including the clinical insights they have fostered.

First of all are those nearly three hundred families from Eastern Kentucky who must remain unnamed, with whom my colleagues and I were privileged to work and consult over the past six years. They are wonderful, unforgettable families. Unnamed also, but equally important, are local community leaders, school superintendents, teachers, physicians, and the staffs of various other service agencies with whom specific clinical and more general regional problems were discussed.

From the outset the assistance of the public health nursing staffs of the four local health departments was indispensable.

We, the traveling component of our clinical team from the University of Kentucky, depended heavily upon the personal qualities and professional skills of the resident nurses in our joint work. Thus, to Iva Brown, Ann Feltner, Ruby Parker, Faye Hensley, Carol Stickney, Myra Stevens, Louise Dunaway, Jo Britton, Beverly D'Angelo, Oda Holliday, Dorothy Yoder, and Sister Mary Glass are due very special thanks. Working with these senior nurses, and with the children and families in the project, were the many nursing students from Berea College, who in their senior year were assigned on a semester rotation to the local health departments for field experience. Under the able leadership of Frances Allen, professor of nursing, the students stimulated all of us by their empathy and enthusiasm.

Every kind of assistance was provided our work by the staff and trainees of the Departments of Psychiatry and Social Work at the University of Kentucky. Miss Leone Renn, director of Social Services, remained keenly interested in the project throughout and provided an unbroken line of psychiatric social workers who, with me and our residents in general psychiatry, junior medical students, and social work students, made the many weekly clinic trips from Lexington to the mountains over the years. It is impossible to do justice to the contributions of each of them. But to caseworkers Dorothy Miller, Albert Johnson, Maryrhea Morelock, Natasha Pfeiffer, Sherry Wathen, Lane Veltkamp, Richard Welsh, and their students I remain clinically and personally indebted. From among our general psychiatry residents, Mary N. Smith, M.D., must be singled out for her initial empathy for the people and their region and for her enthusiasm for the project when she was a trainee. Today, as a faculty member of the Department of Psychiatry, she shares equally with me the clinical-administrative supervision of our work.

That I undertake the writing of the book was suggested initially by Thomas R. Ford, professor and chairman of the Department of Sociology at the University of Kentucky, and by Matthew Hodgson, development editor of the University Press of Kentucky. Professor Ford's long-established, detailed knowledge of the sociology of the Southern Appalachian region had immeasurably facilitated the initiation of our clinical work. There have since been frequent occasions to consult with him with regard to the emerging clinical data and the many interpretations and hypotheses generated from the work. Mr. Hodgson's role has been that of a good and patient, persistent, gentle yet probing caretaker of both author and manuscript as the work of writing proceeded.

Thanks are due also to James Brown, professor of sociology and of rural sociology at the University of Kentucky. He knows the Southern Appalachian region well and contributed generously from that knowledge.

I was fortunate to have Maryrhea Morelock not only as a full-scale professional participant in the project for two years as social worker but also as a critical reviewer of the ideas set forth here. Raised in a small coal-mining camp in the Southern Appalachian region, Mrs. Morelock brought to her professional work abiding empathy and keen insight into her people and her region. She remains invaluable to me as a friend and colleague. Not only has she insisted that I understand her insights, but also that in the process of writing nothing be lost in the translation!

Several other people have contributed immeasurably at various stages in the analysis of the clinical data and during the preparation of the manuscript. But first and last I owe gratitude and apology to my wife Glyndon, son John, and daughter Mary whose initial encouragement reinforced others' suggestions that the book be written and who continued to provide sustaining support through the many months of the manuscript's completion.

To my secretaries, Ernestine Gentry and Charlotte Rice, go thanks for their patient labor in typing the many revisions and final copy of the book.

The names of children and their families in the manuscript were of course altered to insure confidentiality of the clinical information based on their lives.

Finally, I must underscore my debt to the earlier and continuing work of others. In a real sense the Eastern Kentucky region, its unforgettable children and families, and those others who have worked in the region on a long-term basis have contributed much to my own growth and development as a person and as a career child psychiatrist. If in some ways my observations and interpretations recorded here are accurate, it is at once intended as a small tribute to those who have taught me my lessons well, and as my attempt to join them in telling the complex story of a particular people and their development.

D. H. L.

PART I   Troubled
           Children

CHAPTER 1

Appalachian
Themes

Eastern Kentucky first thrust itself
on my awareness when, as a boy of
twelve, I was given a copy of *Names
on the Land*.[1] The author of that book
had drawn together a collection of
unusual names of towns and places
from across the United States. As
a native Northwesterner—from Whidbey Island, in Puget Sound, in the
western part of the state of Washington—I was fascinated by the author's
descriptions of the origins of such
Eastern Kentucky places as Ida May,
Paint Lick, Hell-for-Certain, Bright-
shade, and Asher's Fork. I wondered
then what the people were like who
lived in places with names like these.
   Twenty-five years later I began seeing children and families from these
same towns and hollows and as a by-
product gained fresh insight into my
own earlier provincialism. At twelve
I had considered Eastern Kentucky
names very strange, compared with
the familiar names about me: San de
Fuca, Anacortes, Concrete, Snohom-
ish, and Mukilteo. It was only later,
after prolonged fieldwork in child
psychiatry in Eastern Kentucky, that

I came to understand how much all of us personalize the names we give to where we live.

My second introduction to some aspects of the Southern Appalachian region, of which Eastern Kentucky is an integral part, occurred at about the same time in my boyhood. My father frequently took my mother, my younger brother, and me trout fishing with him in the northern Cascade Mountains wilderness area. To reach this remote section, approximately ninety miles inland from our farm on Whidbey Island, we drove eastward through the fertile flatlands to enter the foothills of the mountains. There, as along the entire western slope of the Cascades in Washington and Oregon, the foothills are quite similar in topography to the coves and hollows of the Southern Appalachian region. The rounded Cascade foothills are heavily forested in Douglas fir, hemlock, and western red cedar. Many of the widely separated valleys are sharply V-shaped. Other valleys are somewhat broader and support scattered subsistence farms in small river and stream bottoms. Only a few roads then penetrated the area.

The scenic western Cascade foothills region, remote and isolated, was thinly populated at the time of my boyhood visits in the late 1930s and early 1940s. Many of the families who did live there had migrated into the area from the Southern Appalachian region. The particular section we traveled through on our fishing trips had been settled by a group of families from western North Carolina, West Virginia, and Eastern Kentucky. The circumstances of the migration of these families and the personal and social characteristics of individual family members served as my early introduction to Southern Appalachian family life, structure, and functioning. The impressions I gained in my childhood were vividly revived when I came to review the sociology of the Southern Appalachian region in 1964 and began to work directly with emotionally troubled children and their families in field mental health clinics in Eastern Kentucky that same year.

One Appalachian migrant family who had settled in the Cascade foothills came to be close friends of our family. We visited them often on our fishing trips in the area. They typified, I feel now, the extremely close, personal attachment that members of Appalachian families have to each other and to the land itself. Kinship ties are strong within these families, not only binding family members to one another over the years but shaping even the migration patterns of those who have left the Southern Appalachian region for other places. Equally as strong as kinship ties is the southern highlander's love of place, of home, of his land. The Jenkins family my family knew were like this.

Doc Jenkins, as I saw when I was introduced to him and his family by my father, was markedly different from our neighbors, the Dutch immigrants who farmed the fertile river flatlands west of the Cascades. Doc, forty then, was a tall, thin man, quite tanned and weathered. His smile, like his soft drawl, was slow to start, but both these features were indicative of the immense inner warmth I came to know. He reminded me, really, of my mother's percolator. Nowhere was his warmth as a person more evident than in his relationships with his children or, as we came to know him through the years, with my younger brother and me. Both of us loved him. His concern for our family was directly, almost tenderly, expressed. Each trip we were plied with gifts of vegetables from his garden, honey from his hives, bacon from the smokehouse, and whitefish from the Skagit River. But, above all, Doc asked his key question: "How are you doing?" Neighbors spoke of Doc as "quiet-turned" and "jubrous"—plucky in Appalachian argot. He worked hard when he wanted to work, loved his family and his place in the foothills, and never turned his back on his neighbors.

Mrs. Jenkins was a short, stocky, warm and bubbly person who seemed to chatter incessantly. She was actually flushed and sweaty much of the time, from the effort of relating so intensely and getting all those words out. It was clear that the family's four-room cabin and the garden were her domain. She and the two daughters, one six and one twelve when I met the family, ran it like a fiefdom. Around the house, Doc and the six boys, who ranged in age from six to nineteen, quietly took their orders from Mrs. Jenkins. Outdoors beyond the garden was their province. The two older boys worked with Doc as seasonal loggers in the local sawmill. With their father all the boys hunted, fished, butchered the hogs, and did their mother's bidding.

The boys, as I remember them, were all fair-haired and blue-eyed like Doc. Unlike their mother, however, they were quite silent and withdrawn from my family when, as visitors, we first knew them. Even in later years, after they had accepted us, they remained relatively silent when we were there. Much of the time their later liking of us was demonstrated in nonverbal ways. One of them might quietly take my brother and me out to the smokehouse to see the new kittens, for example.

By any comparative standard, the Jenkins family was a poor, working-class family. Their annual income, derived from Doc's summer employment as a medical corpsman in an Alaskan salmon cannery and from his and his sons' occasional logging work in the Cascades, was probably less than $2,000. But they lived comfortably. Their house was old and worn but was neat, clean, and weather-tight. They grew, fished, or hunted for most of what they ate. Their social life seemed completely satisfying to them. Quiet visits with their Appalachian migrant neighbors, an occasional box social at the nearby white-framed, one-room Primitive Baptist church, a program put on by the children at the local two-room schoolhouse—such events filled their needs beyond their homelife. The family's way of living was typical of the twenty-nine families, a majority of whom were Appalachian migrants, who had settled in that particular part of the Skagit River valley. Ten of the families were clustered about the general store, garage, restaurant, church, and schoolhouse that made up Rockmount, an unincorporated village. The remainder of the families were strung out along the river road for several miles on either end of town.

By background, Doc Jenkins was one of several older boys of a large coal-mining family in West Virginia who were of English stock. At the beginning of World War I, when he was seventeen, he enlisted in the navy. After "going outside," he was trained as a medical corpsman and served for a time at one of the naval stations in Seattle, Washington. During off-duty hours he began exploring the western Cascade foothills. The coves and hollows reminded him very much of his family's homestead. After the war he returned to West Virginia and married. He tried coal-loading in the mines for a time but was dissatisfied with this, the only work available in the area. Mining was dirty and underground, and he had grown up enjoying the woods and fresh air. Besides, his naval service had introduced him to economic opportunities outside his home region. Finally he decided to leave home and to try his luck elsewhere.

Even in migration, however, earlier regional training shaped Doc's choice of a place to settle. He decided to migrate directly into that particular section of the Cascade foothills that reminded him of West Virginia and that had been settled earlier by a few West Virginia families who were known to him. Doc's love of his people and love of his land were the two determining factors in his choice of the area around Rockmount.

The trip out was made one spring in his old car. Once in the new area, Doc settled his young wife and babies on a part-hillside, part-bottomland subsistence farm of fifteen acres in a bend of the Skagit River a mile east of Rockmount. His place was several hundred yards down the gravel river road from the farm of another West Virginia family. For a time after they arrived Doc worked as a regular logger with the local sawmill, but he found the work too confining, too demanding. To hold a steady job at the mill he was required to adjust to the mill's capricious schedule and demands to check in often at the front office to determine whether work was available that day. During his years in the navy, Doc had chafed under time schedules. He decided at this point to look for other work that permitted him a greater degree of personal independence, that held less rigorously to time schedules, and that did not interfere with his fall hunting and fishing.

Having been trained as a medical corpsman, Doc was able to secure seasonal employment as a first aid man at an isolated salmon cannery on Kodiak Island, Alaska. It was there that he met my father, who was employed in Alaska during the summers by the United States Department of Interior, Bureau of Fisheries, as a salmon conservationist. The two men became fast friends. In the fall of each year both returned to Washington, where the friendship flourished, too.

Years later, after I had begun to conduct fieldwork in Eastern Kentucky, I realized what a valuable gift my boyhood acquaintance with Doc and his family and their way of living had been. Doc's work pattern, for instance: I readily saw how typical it was of the mountain man's love of independence and his aversion to time-oriented, inflexible work schedules.

As I began to meet Eastern Kentucky families, I was reminded again and again of the entire life-style of the Jenkinses and of the warmth of our friendship. I felt far less a stranger in Appalachia than I might logically have expected to feel and much readier to be of some pracical help to the people. In some important ways I was prepared for the youngsters with whom we were going to work through our clinic. There was Cindy, for example—a shy twelve-year-old with a severe school phobia.

I could understand the family forces which, benign in the case of the Jenkinses, could in aberrational form produce the fears that paralyzed the child. I don't mean, of course, that I was able to diagnose and understand her problem on the basis of my own background; I simply mean that I had a sort of head start.

We were going to be working with children—and parents—whose backgrounds and expectations were quite different from those we often sum up as "middle class." There was Eddie, an eight-year-old whose father "pet on" him and, as a deacon in a small country church, spent a good part of his weekends singing at funerals—with Eddie in tow. There was the curly-haired six-year-old who capsuled her psychophysiologic problems: "I get this terrible headache 'cross my eyes and pains in my stomach and then I puke, Buddy." There was the family that kept to its trailer like a turtle in its shell. They were all individual and different, of course. But they were, so to speak, different in a distinct way. They shared a land and a history and a culture. And even when it came to the intense feeling of the people for their land, I felt a kinship, because in Washington I had grown up with as strong a love of place as Southern Appalachian people have for their region. Even so, when we began our clinical work in Eastern Kentucky, I rapidly realized that receptivity to the people was only the beginning of the job.

CHAPTER 2

The
Manchester
Project

The persons I describe and discuss
in this book live in four Eastern Kentucky counties—Clay, Jackson, Lee,
and Owsley. I came into contact
with them through an unusual venture
which we call the Manchester Project
(Manchester is the county seat of Clay
County).

This came into being in 1964,
largely as a result of the initiative
of Mildred Gabbard, the regional
health officer for the four counties,
and her staff of eight senior public
health nurses. In a mountain area
such a public health team is of much
greater relative importance than its
urban counterpart. In the first place,
there are fewer doctors (in some
counties, none at all) per capita. Besides, a high proportion of the patients
are poor, from isolated parts of the
area, and many of them would be
unaware even of the existence of
medical and psychiatric care if they
were not sought out by the nurses.

For some years before 1964, Dr.
Gabbard and her staff had seen the
great need for services for the emotionally troubled children they en-

countered in their traditional health programs. At the time there were no facilities for such children. Fifty-four hospital beds were available for the area's 49,000 people, and the eleven general physicians in the four counties were almost overwhelmed by the overall health needs of a population that included a large group of children (20,000) and the aged. The Kentucky State Hospital at Danville and Eastern State Hospital at Lexington provided once-a-month, brief-contact, after-care clinics in the local health departments for discharged adult psychiatric patients. The only mental health services for children were of an indirect kind, through the Kentucky Department of Child Welfare and the public-assistance programs. These were meager indeed and could hardly have been otherwise.

For these reasons, this very active health team turned to the Department of Psychiatry of the University of Kentucky College of Medicine to ask if we would be interested in working with them to organize and develop mental health services for children in the four-county area. This was both a welcome request and a stimulating one, for we recognized our need to develop formal means for training persons who would later be involved in community mental health programs throughout the state. A field laboratory—a community in which we could evolve a program—would be one answer. The Manchester Project, a genuine joint venture, was the result.

The project began in August 1964. Its primary feature is the operation of weekly child psychiatry clinics in the local health departments of the four counties. These clinics offer diagnostic and treatment services for emotionally troubled children and their families. They also offer regular consultations on children to schools, family physicians, child-welfare and public-assistance workers, Head Start and day-care programs, and training seminars. Project personnel have included the local health department staffs and a traveling component from the University of Kentucky including, in addition to me and another staff psychiatrist, two psychiatric social workers, two third-year residents in general psychiatry on one-year rotation, and several social work trainees on one-semester rotation. Another involved group has consisted of eight to ten senior nursing students from the Department of Nursing of Berea College. For field experience they have been assigned on semester rotation to the local health departments and to the Manchester Project itself.

At the outset of the project we decided to conduct a limited field survey of child development in the region, the aim being to see how Eastern Kentucky families in general rear their children. This step was necessary before we could begin dealing with the problems presented by troubled children. Our study sought to define the normal developmental baseline in this sub-culture; from this we could determine which events represented pathological personality deviations.

Twelve study families were selected by the district public health nurses from their case loads. Two principles guided the selection: the lower, middle, and upper socioeconomic classes were to be equally represented (so that we could determine whether or not specific developmental themes were class-related); the families should be known to the nurses as having reared, and now rearing, children who were regarded as maturing satisfactorily, with no evidence of psychopathology.

I spent a half-day in the home of each of these families.[1] That is how I met the Perkinses. This family, Maggie Perkins especially, had been chosen by the nurses for my review because "they are good people who have normal children; they are honest; they have about a middle income for families in the area; and Maggie is a good talker." All these observations proved to be accurate.

The Perkinses' house stands perhaps a quarter of a mile up a dirt driveway from the main road connecting the two towns in the county. The farm lies partly on a hill and partly on a narrow shelf of bottomland along the Red Bird River. The white frame house on the apron of the hillside is surrounded by old fruit trees and a partially painted white picket fence. The flowers and bushes in the yard give evidence of long-standing care. As I drove up, I saw that the place was neat, although there was a careworn oldness about it. A youngster who turned out to be Scott, age three, was the first to greet me when I drove into the yard. He ran to the edge of the front porch, with a grin peeked at me from behind a post, and then ran from post to post playing hide-and-seek. As I approached the porch he ran and stood near his mother, who greeted me with outstretched hand. Maggie was warm, effusive, and talked spontaneously in an almost constant flow. A short, stocky woman of forty, she, like Doc Jenkins's wife, was flushed with the effort of relating and talking. She was neatly dressed in a cotton print dress and long apron. She had been told of my coming by the nurses, was expecting me, and ushered me to a chair in the front room. She was a sort of woman who "gathered you up and took you in." I was made to feel at home almost immediately.

Herschel Perkins, a lean, weathered man of forty-two, came in from the kitchen. As the interview proceeded, he remained rather shy and deferred to his wife, who was "quite a talker," as he said. He in his turn reminded me very much of Doc Jenkins. Although Herschel spoke little, he listened attentively to his wife's descriptions of how they raised Donald Wayne, eighteen, Dale, six, and Scott, three. Herschel showed pride in his wife, their home, and their children, and later he seemed particularly to enjoy my walking around his farm with him. He showed me his vegetable garden, the smokehouse, the wash house, his bee hives, the hogpen, his two milk cows, and the acre of tobacco being grown as the family's only annual cash crop.

Herschel had been born into a poor coal-mining family in Harlan, Kentucky, but had moved here to this farm in early boyhood. His wife described his background: "My husband grew up here right in this house, on this farm, from the age of five or six. There were seven boys and three girls in his family— ten in all. A lot of the younger children died when they were babies. Herschel was the only one who stayed here and had any interest in working his father's farm. His brothers and sisters went to Cleveland, Nebraska, Covington, and Cincinnati, and there's one teaching school in Kentucky, and another all over in the army."

Maggie told me she had been born in Virginia, but was raised in a coal camp in Floyd County, Kentucky, where her father worked in the mines. When she learned that I was interested in the way she raised her children, she immediately began to compare herself and her mothering role with her own mother. "There was a large family of us—eight while I was growing up. My mother right now has a sixteen-year-old boy who's my brother. We kids would spend summers and things in Virginia when we would go to my grandmother's. I would like to be as good a woman as my mother. I don't feel I'm adequate to do as good as she did with us. She seemed to be such a perfect mother. She was the type of person that you wouldn't want to cross her or disappoint her. She trusted you and let you know she trusted you. You would feel ashamed if you weren't good and did things that would go against her trust. I wouldn't do anything to make her feel disappointed in me. She drilled and talked to us. She told us that all a girl ever had was her reputation. We were raised up poor. I notice a difference between my mother's time and my own. For instance, in my mother's day if a girl had a baby out of wedlock in a mining camp we were not allowed as children to associate ever with her. In mining camps that kind of talk got around very fast about women. Now no one cares whether you talk to such a woman or not."

At this point in the interview we were joined by Maggie's father-in-law, who was neatly dressed in a white shirt, necktie, creased charcoal gray pants, and a gray sleeveless sweater. His white hair was cut in a butch style. He wore rimless glasses and carried a cane. He appeared to be about seventy years old. He was alert, responsive, and filled with pride about his daughter-in-law, his household, his farm, his son Herschel, and his grand-children. With pleasure he showed me a picture of Donald Wayne, the oldest of the Perkinses' three children, who was then stationed at an air base in Texas. He was quietly amused by some of the playful antics of Scott on the front porch before Scott fell off the window ledge and came inside.

From the sheer weight of Maggie's words, it was clear that each of her three children, when a baby, had had a unique place in their family. I gathered pages and pages of verbatim notes as she reviewed in great detail what her children had been like as infants. Feeding, bathing, diapering, burping, crawling, sleeping, and her opinions about articles she had read in *Good Housekeeping* on infant care were covered extensively. Further-more, at one point Maggie corroborated her reminiscent—or historical—focus on her children's infancy by relating to Scott in a manner that at first was appropriate to his age, but later turned infantile manner. What happened was that, while Mrs. Perkins sat on the sofa with her back to the open front-room window, Scott crawled up on the window ledge from the porch to look at me through the window, his head just behind and to the side of his mother's. He fell backward from this perch and began to cry. In a matter-of-fact way Maggie promptly turned and called: "All right, I guess you've fallen and bumped yourself. Come on in here and let me see what it's about." Scott came in at once, stopped crying immediately, and crawled up into his mother's lap, where he remained for the next forty-five minutes. During that time he relaxed against his mother's bosom, occasionally looking up at her and smiling or gazing at me with a studying expression. From time to time he stood up in his mother's lap and walked around on her lower abdomen and thighs or leaned against her shoulder. Maggie permitted this at some discomfort to herself; if Scott blocked her view, she would move her head so that she could look at me as she continued talking. Sometimes she would shift Scott from one side to the other, but she never made a move to put him down. At one point later on, Scott attempted to wriggle off his mother's lap, but Maggie encircled him with her arms, tightened them, and continued to hold him close to her. Scott did not whine, complain, or vocalize at any point during these forty-five minutes. Mother and son remained close, both apparently content, smiling. Maggie described this closeness she had with all her children: "My children are confident—all of them. They never whine or complain. One of us is always there. Mine have always come from the time that they were very little to see where I was—they would come into the kitchen and talk with me. They didn't seem to want to talk to their father or to the older ones so much, but brought their confidences to me."

This interview—both in what the Perkinses told me and in the interactions that I observed—was a particularly thorough portrayal of regional child-development themes that I came to know. Most notably, data from all our interviews yielded the same consistent theme: infancy—the first year and a half of life—shaped the interactional patterns of all these families. Parents, grandparents, and older children freely gave of themselves to infants, who seemed to thrive in every way.

These relationships with infants were highly permissive and indulgent. But beginning with the motor-muscular (after eighteen months) and preschool stages of development, parental attitudes changed rapidly and progressively. We saw less and less of what we considered age-appropriate involvement in children's attempts to master tasks, and parents devoted correspondingly less interview time to discussing these later stages. The local nurses put it succinctly: "We've known all along that children here sort of grow up on their own after they're babies."

As they began to use the autonomy that the development of motor-muscular skills makes possible, these children, when they were actually out of sight, were often treated by their parents as though they no longer existed. As a result they frequently toddled into situations of real or potential danger. But when the children were close by, parents generally displayed the overprotective, indulgent, permissive behavior characteristic of the children's infancy. Maggie Perkins's handling of Scott is of course a perfect example. Scott's response to her treatment is equally typical. The children in general reacted with similar infantile modes of adjustment—clinging, whining, demanding, basking with pleasure at being babied.

What seems to be the case is that the parents saw the child's emerging autonomy as a threat to their complete domination and possession of him, and they dealt with the threat simply by denying it. When the child did come to them, this was taken as a sign that he wanted them in their familiar caretaking role. This infantilizing point of view is often expressed in casual conversation by Eastern Kentucky women, as when they say of children as old as five or six: "What beautiful babies!"

My observations of the way mountain families focus on their children's infancy parallel Jack Weller's conclusions. "Babies have a unique place in the mountain family. Though the mountain man often pays little attention to the large children, he will make a great deal of fuss over babies, playing with them, fondling them, and carrying them about. . . . Children are highly valued, because they give meaning to the parents' lives. One mother expressed it: 'If I didn't have my children, I wouldn't have nothin'.' Another, speaking of her nine-year-old son, her only child, said, 'Yes, I dress him and tie his shoes. It's my pleasure to do it as long as he's at home.' "[2] As children grow, adults largely cease to play with them, supervise them inappropriately, and furnish no positive models for training in setting limits on impulses, for establishing disciplinary controls, or for training in age-appropriate relating to or talking with other adults. Toddlers and preschool children are shoved off to play when someone calls; they are not allowed to interrupt the adults' conversation. Disciplinary training is set in the same mode: adults generally notice the misbehavior of children, usually in public, only when the situation is beyond the point at which an adult could have intervened to set the training model for the child's more effective mastering of his feelings, impulses, and relationships. Instead, misbehavior is allowed to come to a head, and physical punishment is meted out swiftly and sternly as a consequence. I noted these patterns more in families of the very poor and the working class, but found that in a somewhat attenuated way they held true for the middle and upper classes as well.

I was particularly struck by the extremely limited training in verbal skills that the children received, whatever their ages. This nonverbal theme was also most prominent in very poor and working-class families. I rarely saw books, magazines, or even newspapers in these homes. The poor, of course, had no money to buy them, but their own lack of formal education had led them also to place little value on verbal skills. Talk in their homes was sparse. Rarely was there anything to read except a few papers the children brought home from school. But parents did not encourage the children to read even this material to them. Moreover, in an attenuated way the same theme prevailed for many middle-income families in the counties. Even families like the Perkinses, good talkers, did not read to their children or read only infrequently. And these parents did not reinforce their children's school training in reading by asking the children to read to them at home. This theme found vivid expression, I felt, in the fact that rarely did an Eastern Kentucky middle-class child of late preschool or school age show me his drawings, school papers, or books as an initial display of his skills, in the manner frequent among urban middle-class children. Instead, the Appalachian child more often than not wanted me to see what he could do in some action-oriented game. In addition, I noted frequently during my visits to first and second grades in county elementary schools that standard reading texts, like *Dick and Jane,* popular in urban schools in middle-class areas, furnished an experiential model, around which words were constructed, that was completely dissimilar to the life experiences of many mountain children.

One further, consistently recurring theme in my review of these families merits attention. I refer here to the evidences of infantile sexuality, long known to most mothers and nursemaids, that are normally observed in preschool children. Most Eastern Kentucky mothers could not talk spontaneously about this important area of their children's development. Nor could they do so in response to my gently put but direct questions about children's curiosity concerning sexual differences, masturbation, genital exhibiting, pregnancy and where babies come from, and the like. Even a talker like Maggie Perkins, who spontaneously had filled my field notebooks with comments on her children's infancy, had only this to say in response to prolonged questions in the area of the children's sexual maturation and functioning: "My children never really asked me much—

about that. I can't remember them ever handling themselves. I've read about others doing that—mine never did—or maybe I just didn't see it. I believe living on a farm they just naturally understand more about nature, like with cattle, than kids in the city." Maggie, previously relaxed and comfortable in discussing other areas of her children's growth, was singularly uncomfortable in my probing into sexual development. She was not alone in this particular discomfort—it remained a consistent theme with other families in the region as well.

Overall, my brief study of Eastern Kentucky child-development practices underscored three prominent training themes. First, families strongly emphasize (overemphasize, I feel) the infancy of their children. This is, I believe, an expression of the desire to keep families close-knit and results from the familistic orientation of Appalachian families, which has been observed by numerous commentators, notably Thomas R. Ford and Jack Weller. Ford advances an interesting hypothesis on this point, namely, that the inability of many poor Southern Appalachian families to provide for their members' basic needs leads to an increasing "closure" of the family system. The less the family provides, the more insecure the members become; the more insecure they become, the more they turn inward to their traditional source of security—the family itself. Thus the poorer families, in particular, continue to foster closeness, often in inappropriate ways, as the children grow older.

The second theme is the marked lack of emphasis on developing verbal skills. The third is the fact that sexual maturation and functioning, whether one is considering adults or children, is virtually a tabooed topic. As we began our consulting work we began to see how these themes found reflection in the mental health and mental disorder of the region's children.

CHAPTER 3   Power
of the
Family

One day the University of Kentucky
Medical Center admitted Lonnie
Thompson, a gaunt, fifty-two-year-old
coal miner from Eastern Kentucky.
Lonnie was sent to Lexington by his
local physician for review of his
chronic obstructive airway disease—a
disorder that in recent years has become widely known as coal miners'
black lung.

When he was placed on the specialty ward, Lonnie found himself
separted from the family members
and friends who had brought him to
Lexington. After several days had
passed, days in which he became increasingly anxious, he found himself
trapped in an extremely unfamiliar
situation: a number of physicians and
other persons in long white coats had
placed him on a table in a strange
room and had shut the door. They
stood about him, apparently discussing his condition in words that were
themselves quite strange. Then they
began to undress him.

At this point, Lonnie became dis-
oriented. He spoke confusedly, mut-
tering something about seeing a

"white cocoon." The medical team immediately dropped the planned procedures and called on a psychiatrist for an emergency consultation.[1] It was a while before Lonnie could speak coherently. Then he described his overwhelming terror at being in the strange surroundings, in the hands of strange people. He had felt caught, with no way out. The only thing he knew to do was to pray for "grace." And that grace came in the form of a large, white blanket, like a cocoon, that descended from the ceiling and wrapped itself around him. With this protection, he had felt somewhat less frightened.

Lonnie's altered perceptions and projection of the white cocoon were understood by the psychiatrist as an acute dissociative or conversion reaction, adaptive in those particular circumstances in the sense that it allowed him to cope at the moment with a terrifyingly unfamiliar situation. But what made it so terrifying?

The answer is directly relevant to the planning of the Manchester Project. At the University of Kentucky Medical Center we frequently see that patients from mountain areas are almost overwhelmed by the scattered specialized facilities and by what they view as the impersonal institutionalized services. Certainly few persons become as frightened as Lonnie or go to such psychological extremes in defending themselves, but his experience is essentially a dramatic version of a common reaction. For basic reasons, Appalachian families tend to differ from the majority of Americans, who want to and therefore can accept health-care service wherever it is available.

At the outset of our project, the local health officer and her nursing staff discussed these local attitudes toward health care and some of their underlying causes. They gave several compelling reasons that the mental health field clinics for children should be based in the local health departments. First, there was the trend for families to gravitate to the local health departments for their other health needs. Because of the traditional primacy of extended-family or kinship ties, a family's acceptance of any health service depended upon their acceptance of the person who gave the service.

Second, these Eastern Kentucky families shared certain characteristics in their attitudes toward health care: they reacted to symptoms of disease and to the idea of disease itself with strong fears and anxieties. Many families, having little education and low income, hampered by barriers of language, were all too often confused, overly apprehensive, or even overwhelmed by health problems. Because of the traditional tendency of the Southern Appalachian individual to attempt to cope with anxiety by turning inward upon his close family system, only a health-care person long known and familiar could be accepted in a helping role.

The senior public health nurses understood this highly important familistic orientation. These nurses had flexibility in time and schedules, the mobility to reach people in isolated areas, and, above all, a visible proximity to the people who needed their services. In addition, their understanding of the culture equipped them for social encounter and interaction. Though themselves in the middle and professional classes, the nurses were generally products of the cultural background of their people. They could therefore establish rapport with their people much more easily than could other middle-class professionals. Accordingly, the public health nurses, working through various health services, could counter or offset the traditional reluctance of many Appalachian families to seek help in problem-solving from outside agencies or clinics.

These points cannot be overstressed, so crucial are they for the planning and delivery of all types of health services in Eastern Kentucky. I suspect these factors are crucial as well in the wider Southern Appalachian region. In effect, many Appalachian families lack the psychological mobility that would lead them to seek specialized health care outside their local communities. They cooperate far better in extended health care if it is offered by familiar persons in a familiar setting.

It was for these reasons, as well as for those involving time, economic, and transportation factors, that the staffs of the local health departments had for years encouraged the development of a variety of special health clinics within the health departments. Multiphasic screening of preschool and early school-age children was conducted locally. Regional pediatric clinics, staffed by the resident nurses and a traveling group of pediatricians, pediatric residents, interns, medical students, and social workers, had been established on a quarterly basis in the county health departments of much of Eastern Kentucky. Similarly, regional cardiology and neurology clinics were developed. In this respect, then, the establishment of the Manchester Project's field mental health clinics for children in the four local health departments followed a regional pattern established somewhat earlier by other specialty clinics.

In our jointly planned and established work with emotionally troubled children and their families, we deliberately sought to use the diagnostic-treatment services of the familiar and accepted public health nurse. We deliberately took our place with other public health programs in the region. In a sense, we rode for acceptance on the coattails of the nurses, who, long familiar to the families we served together, were called by their first names. When we would first meet with an understandably anxious new family that had been referred to one of our field clinics, we would frequently hear something like: "Faye came by to see me, Doctor. She said the teachers over at Gilbert's Creek have been r'iled by Sammy. Faye brought me today. She says it's all right to talk to you." This was typical. The considerable extent to which we were able to win the trust and cooperation of individual patients and their families was due, first and foremost, to the nurses' understanding of the families we served together. They had, in advance, personalized our clinics. No family got service from a stranger.

Repeatedly, in every phase of our work, we found it almost impossible to overemphasize the significance of familism. Its influence was constantly reflected in our clinical experience. In the years since 1964, I have never ceased to be struck by the close, remarkably interdependent functioning of Eastern Kentucky families. Emphasis on extensive kinship ties was the most obvious expression of this familistic orientation. Tiny preschoolers would say in clinic interviews: "Doctor, Sam's my first cousin. He's my daddy's *kin*." *Kin* was the key word we heard everywhere, from young and old alike.

Of particular importance, as we saw in the clinics, was the relationship between this familism and the children's (and families') view of the schools and what was to be expected of them. In earlier years, the schools in Appalachia were direct expressions of the values held by the people: like the people they served, the schools were inner-directed, isolated, and generally poor. Louise Gerrard wrote about these early schools as follows:

"Teacher" often lived in the community, in a home distinguished from its neighbors' by a wooden fence, or by a particularly large collection of plants on the front porch. "Teacher" was probably married to a disabled miner, or a postman, or a clerk in the local store. This hollow was home to her and she wasn't planning to go off somewhere else. Everyone knew her, and she knew everyone.

Johnny wasn't really a wild boy—just high-spirited like all the Kincaids. Sara needed special attention now that her mother was doing poorly and there were all those brothers and sisters to make do for. Isaiah had to be pushed, but once he got going he'd be all right, and as for Ed, she'd tell his daddy the boy wasn't working as hard as Blankenships usually did.

"Teacher" was little different from those around her. Her accent was the same, her speech filled with the same localisms, and although she had more education than most in the area, it was apt to be very little more.[2]

The highly personalized nature of these early local schools—their emphasis on persons and relationships—was quite in accordance with the mountaineer's view of the world. But now the world, and Appalachia with it, has changed. The trend in Eastern Kentucky is toward consolidated schools, at all levels, in all counties. Every year more and more of the isolated schools in neighborhood hollows are being closed.

But the great changes that have brought economic and educational advance to many people in the region have had little impact on many of the lower-class families. Their isolation—geographic, economic, cultural—remains their most notable characteristic as a people, distinguishing them from their more fortunate working-class and middle-class fellows. Nowhere do the differences show up more cruelly than in the classrooms of the consolidated schools. As Louise Gerrard says:

According to modern standards, the children [in small isolated local schools] are getting a very poor education, and clearly it was the duty of county officials to get the children out of the hollows and into better educational institutions.

But somewhere along the line violence was done to local traditions and the needs of the children and their parents. Consolidated schools often meant domination by town children with more manners and charm. Hollow youngsters were thrust upon teachers they did not know, middle class teachers, or at least with middle class ways and aspirations, who resented their assignments, preferring the neat, predictable town children. The accustomed familiarity and tolerance were gone. Being a Kincaid or a Blankenship no longer counted with a teacher who could see no further than the patched trousers or hand-me-down dress. From an informal society they were now in an institutionalized setting where standards of performance were set by the book and deviation often considered intolerable by the teacher. You no longer called her "Teacher"—she was Miss Something or other with a college education, representative of the outside world, and you were just another child.

All too frequently the lower class children's education did not improve appreciably in the new school, for they were considered slow-learners, dull, unmotivated. It became easier and easier for many of them to use the bad roads and lack of bus facilities as an excuse to stay away from the strange new school, and the more they stayed away, the more difficult their academic adjustment became. Soon, some were in little more than caretaker classes, and it seemed to be taken for granted that the "hollow kids" were marking time until old enough to drop out.[3]

Today in Eastern Kentucky, very real problems are involved in reaching and teaching lower-class children. Many such problems were presented in our clinics. Similar ones face teachers of Southern Appalachian migrant children from poor families.

CHAPTER 4

In the Clinic:
Dependency Themes

Eastern Kentucky families are markedly inner-directed. Certainly interdependent functioning characterized
the great majority of our clinic families. Thomas Ford has pointed to an
aspect of this functioning that has
very important implications for mental
health. He observes that the Southern Appalachian family system is held
together by norms of obligation and
not necessarily by bonds of affection.
This of course does not mean that
affection is generally lacking, but
rather that a family member still has
strict obligations to other family members even though he may no longer
feel any affection toward them. And
Ford comments that inner-directedness resulting from an overriding
sense of obligation to each other im-
poses on family members guilt-laden
stresses that tighten closure of the
family system.

Such a close system has a profound
effect on the children. For them, it is
a type of training climate in which
they are taught, in both verbal and
nonverbal ways, to maintain the
system itself, even at the expense of
their own personal and social mat-

uration. We have commonly found that the individual's own growth and development is subordinated to the prime task of maintaining the family as a close unit.

Clearly related to this close, interdependent family functioning, we have come to believe from our clinical work, is the great frequency with which separation anxiety is the emotional conflict faced by individual children and by their parents. Of all their troubles, disruptions in parent-child and other family relationships—whether actual, threatened, or symbolic—caused them the most concern. And not only are separation anxieties and concerns as such frequently found in our clinic families, they undergird a wide variety of other emotional disturbances in the children. That is, crucial focal conflicts involving separation themes can be found in various kinds of psychopathology in these children.

On the basis of our work, we concluded that separation conflicts were prominent in those many children having acute and chronic school-phobic reactions; in those overly dependent children with chronic learning and behavior problems; in those preschool children with deviations in social development or training problems associated with independence and autonomy; in a relatively pure form of symbiotic psychosis in three young children; and in the many children having various psychophysiologic reactions. It is also true that separation concerns are similarly prominent in those children having what I call the "consolidated-school syndrome."

Closely allied to the prevalent theme—the obligation felt by family members to remain close and to avoid real or threatened separation—was the mutual tendency of many children and parents to prolong infantile modes of adjustment beyond the actual period of infancy. One expects infants—even toddlers—to be heavily dependent upon others for care and support, but difficulties ensue if this mode of mutual relating continues relatively unchanged into the later preschool period. These difficulties involve not only how children relate with each other and with grownups but also how autonomously they can begin to master a variety of activities. Many of the Eastern Kentucky families we followed placed strong emphasis on training in obligatory closeness, on training in avoiding separation that would threaten the close family system, and on training attempts, often relatively successful, to maintain their children as babies. Such training really represents an exaggerated degree of, or pathogenic overuse of, the focus on infancy that we noted in our survey of Eastern Kentucky child development.[1]

In these overly close families we were sometimes able to identify specific, relatively pathogenic child-rearing techniques in broad outline. But technique is not the prime factor; more of our family data support the view that unhealthy parental attitudes, sometimes explicit and operating within the parents' awareness, sometimes covert or even unconscious, are more significant in their .crippling effects on the child's personality development than any single child-rearing technique or its specific timing or dosage. Further, we felt that clusters of child-rearing closeness techniques were outgrowths of or were associated with these unhealthy attitudes of the parents. Taken together, parental attitudes and techniques related to closeness, operating over a sufficiently prolonged early childhood training period, seemed to be involved in the various life-styles of these children and their later emotional disturbances.

What our data, therefore, seem to suggest is that a more or less readily identifiable pattern of personality training in closeness operates in many Eastern Kentucky families, leading the children to develop emotional disorders based on related separation anxiety and threatened infantile dependency. Our work also suggests that some specific kinds of parent-child relationships tend to produce certain specific disorders.

ACUTE AND CHRONIC SCHOOL-PHOBIC REACTIONS

Nearly 20 percent of the total case load in the Manchester Project's clinics over the six-year period consisted of children having either an acute or a chronic school phobia. A problem of this magnitude cannot be easily overlooked—the numbers of children involved have simply been too great.

The typical acute disorder occurred in an intelligent, sensitive boy or girl in a Head Start program or one of the lower elementary grades, though children of all ages and grades were involved. The child suddenly developed school fears that deepened into an acute panic state, with physiologic symptoms of this intense anxiety, and refused to attend school. Commonly this happened at the beginning of the school year, after a vacation period, or after a prolonged absence from school later in the year. Seldom could this acutely disturbed child leave home to attend school—the apparent, often stated, object of his dread.

The child who managed to fight his fears sufficiently to leave home often developed further symptoms once in the classroom. Understandably concerned, his teachers often sent him home as too physically ill to attend school. They told the parents that the child could no longer be managed in the classroom. Equally harassed parents—worn to exhaustion by their futile attempts to coax, bribe, threaten, or punish their child back to school—were soon only too ready to yield and keep him at home. And once he was at home, his panic and symptoms subsided abruptly and he remained generally free of symptoms unless an attempt was made to send him back to school.

Confronted with the acutely anxious child, his distraught parents, and his frustrated teachers, the family physician found himself in the middle of a crisis. He frequently concluded that the child was too upset to return to school and granted him home leave for the remainder of the term by signing a request for a homebound teacher. But convalescence failed to solve the problem; the child's symptoms returned with renewed vigor when attempts were made to send him back at the beginning of the next school year. At this point the family physician and the public health nurse directed the case to our mental health clinic. Later on, as school phobia came to be recognized more in the area, referrals were made earlier, often shortly after the initial outbreak of symptoms.

The cases of school phobia referred to us at an early stage were considered as acute emotional emergencies. The problem affected both boys and girls. We defined the problem, as do others,[2] as partial or total inability to attend school resulting from a child's unrealistic fear of some aspect of the school situation. The child often indicated he was afraid of his teacher, or the bully on the bus, or a coming examination. Some children added to this their dread of waiting for the bus in the dark and cold, half a mile down the dirt path leading from their cabin to the county gravel road. The fear was generally accompanied by physiologic symptoms of anxiety (headache, nausea, vomiting, stomachache) or even panic, when school attendance was imminent. Sometimes this panic took the form of acute anxiety attacks, called "smothering spells" by the children and their parents, and terminated in fainting episodes, called "black-out spells" or "falling-out spells."

Unlike the truant, the school-phobic child was generally an intelligent, perfectionistic, hard-driving, achieving youngster who wished he could attend school. The very fact that he could not attend emphasized his inability to leave home, and this inability eventually alerted the family physician, the teacher, the parents, and our team to the fact that the manifest reason for the symptoms (something each child said he feared in the school situation) was not the actual cause. Rather, the child for various reasons had come to fear leaving home, and he attempted to cope with his intense separation concerns by displacing them onto elements of the school situation. Thus we saw separation anxiety as the emotional hub, or primary focal conflict, in all school-phobia situations.

Acute Traumatic School Phobia

The sudden onset of the typical traumatic or common type of acute school phobia had all the characteristics of an emotional crisis mutually involving the child and his family. The crisis was usually brought about by, or followed by, some threat to the child's unusually close, dependent ties to his family. In most cases this threat, or precipitating event, was real and apparent, involving some sudden change in the external circumstances of the child's living that brought intense separation anxiety sharply into focus, changes such as a move, a death, or the illness of a member of the family. The stories of Justin and Sammy show the characteristically dramatic onset of the traumatic or common type of acute school phobia we encountered, its clinical features, and the underlying emotional dynamics involved.

Justin, a shy eleven-year-old fourth grader, was the oldest of the numerous children of a family living on a small farm. In June 1966 he sustained a skull fracture when he fell from a swinging bridge into a dry creek bottom. He was treated then, and through the summer, on the neurosurgical service of the University of Kentucky Medical Center. The doctors removed some bone splinters and capped the hole in his head with a piece of stainless steel. By the time school reopened that fall, Justin was neurologically well; he was quite active and physically able to attend school.

But during the first week of classes he became more and more fearful of leaving home to go to school. His increasing anxiety was somatized, showing up in a variety of ailments: he developed a sleep disturbance, he was nauseated and vomited at breakfast time, and he complained of a sore throat, headache, and abdominal and leg pains. He resisted all the worried attempts of his parents to reassure him, reason with him, or force him into attendance.

As we were able to see, Justin was unconsciously using his somatic complaints as a device to remain at home: the daytime symptoms cleared up completely once he was assured that he did not have to go to school. But, like many other acute school-phobic children, he soon developed other phobic symptoms. He became fearful of animals and noises at night, and he had frequent nightmares.

Another example of acute school phobia is provided by the story of Sammy, a freckled, boisterous six-year-old, the only child of working-class parents who lived in one of the area's small towns. Sammy developed his phobic reaction when he entered the first grade a month after his mother had been hospitalized for an acute cerebral hemorrhage. The end point of his separation concerns was—typically—that his invalid mother would die while he was at school. These frightening fantasies filled his mind as he lay in bed at night, preventing him from going to sleep. They preoccupied him at school the first few troubled days of the term before his anxieties kept him from attending altogether. As soon as the decision was made for him to stay at home, he lost his symptoms, and he spent much of the day bringing aspirin and coffee to his mother in a magical attempt to improve her health.

In each of these children, as was generally the case, school phobia was precipitated by some factor or factors that threatened his security, brought on intense separation anxiety, and increased his dependency needs. Further examination of the school-phobic children we saw indicated that in each case the anxiety in the child triggered equally intense fears of separation in the parents, especially in the mother. Her concerns usually involved a close, primary tie with the child which was threatened by separation. Karen, a six-year-old, and her mother typified these mutual separation concerns. Each was an overreactive worrier, and the two propped each other up like bean poles. Karen became acutely phobic immediately on entering the first grade. Two months earlier her mother had separated from her father in Detroit and moved herself and Karen back to the mountain county to be near the maternal grandmother.

When they first came to the clinic, Karen was quite frightened at being separated from her mother for interviews. The mother, who was seen in a different room by the social worker, anxiously wrung her hands and wondered "what the doctor was doing with Karen." After drying her tears that first time, Karen drew me a picture of a fall scene: leaves with "sad faces" were falling from a nearly barren tree. "The leaves are sad because they left home." And also: "The tree is sad because the leaves are nearly all gone."

Occasionally the mother's separation fears were a defense against her underlying anger toward the child. The parents, now immobilized by their own concerns, served only to intensify the child's difficulty with separation. To cope with their own anxiety, they were all too ready to seize upon the child's somatic complaints and his declared dread of school as an adequate excuse for him to remain at home. Though they often reassured the child and insisted that he attend school, their own separation fears quickly undermined and sabotaged these attempts. This undermining often took the form of contradictory verbal and behavioral cues from one or both parents. For instance, the mother might state that the child really had nothing to fear, but the anxious tone of her voice would readily communicate to the child that disaster awaited him if he left her side. So tightly were the family and child bound together in mutual separation concerns that we often felt that "the umbilical cord pulls at both ends!" Early developmental histories of these children indicated that these separation concerns were a significant part of family training. For example, Justin's parents rather anxiously hovered over him from birth. They overprotected their first child by constantly doing for him tasks he should have been doing for himself. They remained concerned about his climbing trees, riding his bicycle on the county dirt road, or playing near the creek. After the convalescence following his head-injury, Justin and his parents were told by the neurosurgeon that he was well and was able to be active without any restrictions. But Justin wasn't convinced: the trauma and the background of his infantilized development left him anxiously doubtful of his abilities and bodily integrity. One day he graphically demonstrated his feelings. He brought in a dixie cup, containing a thrush's egg gently cradled in cotton. One end of the egg was slightly broken. Justin commented, "It fell out of the mother bird's nest, and got hurt. If you hold it very, very carefully, something else may not happen to it!"

Justin's concern triggered off a rush of anxious injunctions from both his parents that he must not be active. They cautioned him to stay out of trees and off his bike lest he fall again. They encouraged him to remain near them and never out of their sight. The school-phobic reaction that followed was a logical extension of this mutually agreed-upon fear of distance or separation, defensively handled by mutual closeness.

In Sammy's early years, his parents had not been significantly overprotective of him. But his mother was quite dependent, leaning heavily on her own mother and her husband. In addition, she chronically complained of a variety of aches and pains. After her stroke she was quite anxious, often saying that her new condition "will be the death of me yet!" It was not difficult to understand Sammy's intense separation anxiety when school threatened to take him from his "dying" mother's side.

At a deeper level, it was evident that these children could not leave home because they were anxious about what might occur during their absence. This fear was sometimes based on reality, but the child and the parents had overreacted to the situation. In other families we saw, school-phobic children were overconcerned that their quarreling parents would separate, that fathers would injure mothers during a quarrel, that fire or flood would demolish the family's house, or that they would lose the only surviving parents after the others had died or left the home. In a few instances, the precipitating factors were not apparent on the surface. They were more subtle, as in the story of the child who secretly harbored hostile-murderous thoughts toward a new brother and needed to remain at home to undo such thoughts—to see that nothing happened to that brother.

Chronic School Phobia

In these children the fear of school—and of separation from home and family—persisted for months and even years after the initial onset of symptoms. As a result, the children not only had their education seriously disrupted but suffered from marked inability to adjust in all other situations outside their home. In these chronic cases the family relationships generally tended to be more disturbed than those we had noted in the acute traumatic group. The underlying emotional dynamics remained the same in nature but were usually more severe. No family underscored these dynamics more, we felt, than did Cindy, an only child, and her parents. Cindy, a willowy, blond, shy twelve-year-old child of a marginal-farm family in Eastern Kentucky, was severely and chronically phobic. She had never been able to leave home to attend school and had been tutored by a homebound teacher for the past six years. She and her parents seldom left their home, remaining isolated, suspicious, and fearful of outsiders. They had through the years resisted mutually the sporadic attempts to intervene by their primary physician, public health nurses, and mental health personnel. The family was a markedly interdependent one: Cindy's father had never been able to break away geographically or emotionally from his mother. He built a small cabin for his family at the rear of his mother's garden. The threatening quality to them of almost everything in the outside world was reinforced by the father's earlier mining accident and later pneumoconiosis (black-lung disease) and Cindy's congenital heart defect. She had been followed for years in a regional pediatric cardiology clinic, but the family anxiously avoided the recommended hospitalization of Cindy for cardiac catheterization and other studies which might lead to corrective surgery. They put the brief separation involved in hospitalization in overreactive terms: "Cindy will die there!" As the years passed, all family members anxiously clung to one another at home. They actively resisted the attempts of many health personnel to help them with their fears.

Sometimes Eastern Kentucky children with extremely close family ties did not became overtly fearful of attending school as youngsters and adolescents, but developed phobic symptoms only later on, as they left structured ties to family, friends, and church to settle elsewhere. Elsie, who at the time of her referral to our clinic by her family physician was twenty-four, unmarried, living at home, and working as a bank clerk, had earlier developed an acute school-phobic reaction when, at eighteen, she left her family to attend a small college fifty miles from her home. Up to that time she had always been a sweet, dutiful, obedient youngster who stayed within the bosom of her close-knit family and offered no objection to the strict upbringing given by her religious, duty-oriented parents. Her older brothers had made a successful break with home: two of them were Baptist ministers like their father and had settled, after marriages, in small working-class communities along the Ohio River.

After the outbreak of her school phobia six years before she came to us, Elsie had returned home. Her symptoms subsided, only to recur whenever she tried to reenroll in college or to move to another community to do secretarial work. Finally she had given up trying to leave home altogether. In fact, the chronic nature of her severe separation concerns led to significant spreading of her fears about leaving home. By the time of her clinic referral at twenty-four, she had come to dread, and consequently avoided, driving a car, shopping, attending church regularly, dating—any thing that took her from her parents and grandparents with whom she lived. Eventually the health problems of the older members of her family had become an additional source of worry for Elsie. It was after her grandfather's death from a stroke that her anxieties and fears mounted to the point that she became psychotically depressed for a brief time. She was hospitalized, recovered fully from the depressive reaction, and then, on referral, began five long years of discussions with me about her separation problems. It was nearly four years before she could bring herself to admit that her homebound life was not altogether satisfying to her, that she wanted more separated, autonomous functioning for herself.

Even though she continues to live at home and does not date, Elsie over the intervening years has achieved a measure of separation for herself. She no longer places herself at the beck and call of her parents and often leaves them to perform as a singer in her church and to lead Sunday school youth groups there. In addition, she has learned to drive a car and has perfected her creative sewing ability. Mastering skills on her own has given her real satisfaction. She herself once described her improved but still-present separation concerns in these words: "I can still feel it's a sin to cross your folks—to do differently. The Bible says to honor your father and your mother and I sure do that—a lot, I guess. But when I try to get away too far I still get all tense and sad inside, like when I went away to school. I guess I'll never be able to go away real far. I've gone about as far, maybe, as I can go."

Data on School-Phobic Children in Eastern Kentucky
During the period between July 1964 and December 1967, we saw thirty-two children who had acute or chronic school phobias. These children were nearly a fifth of our clinic case load of 166 families. Eighteen children were acutely phobic; fourteen were chronically phobic. In the group of eighteen children with acute school phobia, there were ten boys (ages 7-15) and eight girls (ages 6-12). Three boys and five girls were

age 6 or 7, with the onset of phobic symptoms in the first or second grade. Three boys and three girls were ages 9-12, with the onset of symptoms in the third, fourth, or fifth grade. Four boys were ages 13-15, with the onset of symptoms in the eighth, ninth, or tenth grade. Thirteen children in the group were from intact two-parent families; five children were living with mothers or maternal grandmothers in homes broken by separation, divorce, or death of the father. One-half of the families were of the lower class; one-half were middle-income families by local county standards. Sibling order of these children varied widely. In all the cases there was a clearly discernible event that served as a precipitating stress in the onset of symptoms.

All eighteen children were referred to the Manchester Project's child psychiatry clinic between two weeks and five months after the onset of their school phobia; a majority were referred within one to two months. Fourteen (seven boys, seven girls) successfully underwent brief, crisis-oriented psychological treatment, returning to classes on a regular basis within one to two weeks from the time treatment was begun. The four treatment failures (three boys, one girl) in this group—measured by inability of the child to return to school—were in families who abruptly discontinued clinic contacts. These four families were generally more emotionally unstable and were functioning under a greater degree of separation concern than the fourteen families rated as having successful therapeutic outcomes.

In the group of fourteen children with chronic school phobia, there were seven boys (ages 7-17) and seven girls (ages 10-18). Eleven children were from intact, two-parent families; three children were living with their mothers in broken homes. The chronically phobic children were similar to those in the acute group in socioeconomic class, in the variability of sibling order, and in the fact that a definable precipitating event was discernible in their histories at the onset of symptoms. Five boys and two girls had had onset of phobic symptoms in the first or second grade; three girls had had onset of symptoms in the third or fourth grade. Two boys and two girls had been attending the sixth, eighth, or ninth grade when symptoms began. All these children were referred for treatment late in the course of their phobic disorders. Seven children had symptoms from one to three years before referral; seven children were referred from three to seven years after the initial onset of symptoms. One or more of several factors accounted for late treatment or late referral for treatment of this group: the school and the families were late in consulting the local primary physician; some local school systems had a policy either of not requiring children to attend school or of not enforcing school attendance; some phobic children were known to the primary physician early in the course of their disorder, but the physician lacked the time, the knowledge, or the desire to treat these cases himself; for a time in the past, in the absence of any mental health facilities for children in Eastern Kentucky, primary physicians had no treatment resource to which they could refer cases they could not treat themselves.

Whatever combination of these or other factors accounted for late referral of each of these fourteen chronically phobic children, the treatment results were uniformly poor. Of the fourteen children, thirteen failed to return to school. The one child who did return was a shy, moderately retarded sixteen-year-old boy, who, following two months of psychiatric hospitalization for an acute schizophrenic reaction that developed one year after the outbreak of school-phobic symptoms, continued in a combined outpatient psychotherapeutic and work-study vocational rehabilitation program. Ten of the fourteen families abruptly broke off treatment contacts after a few weeks, apparently accepting the chronic nature of their children's school-phobic problems. The remaining three families continued treatment contacts inconsistently for a few months, then drifted away from the clinic.

Importance of Early Treatment

The project's relative success with the acutely school-phobic children seemed to be related to two interacting factors: early referral and treatment, and less intense family emotional pathology in the fourteen successfully treated cases, compared with more intense separation fears in the four families unsuccessfully treated. In the early cases, it seemed we were dealing with families in an acute emotional crisis but before a more crippling emotional disorder had developed. There was a striking relationship between the promptness with which treatment was begun and the remission of the acute symptoms in these fourteen children. When treatment was initiated shortly after the symptoms appeared, school attendance was resumed within a few weeks.

In both the acute and the chronic groups, neither the age

of the child, the child's sex, his grade at the onset of symptoms, nor the nature or intensity of the precipitating stress was significant in determining the outcome of treatment.

By contrast, results with the group of chronic cases showed that when treatment was postponed as long as a year after the onset of the phobia, return to school became much more difficult to achieve. Thirteen of the fourteen children in this group never returned to school. When the problem had persisted for a long period of time without being successfully resolved, the children and their families resorted to a more regressive solution which was more difficult to modify. The outcome of treatment with the acute and chronic school-phobic children we saw in Eastern Kentucky compares with Waldfogel's and Gardner's findings with a similar group of children in Boston.[3]

On the basis of this experience with school-phobic children, Mary N. Smith and I have published an article focusing on treatment techniques that family physicians and public health nurses can use in helping children with acute phobias.[4] Because school phobia is such a significant emotional problem among Eastern Kentucky children, we wanted to underscore the need for early case-finding and to outline ways community personnel can help these children. This is particularly pertinent in light of the fact that few Southern Appalachian counties have mental health clinics to which such children can be referred.

OVERLY DEPENDENT PERSONALITY DISORDERS

A moderate number of school-age boys and girls (ages 6-12) with chronic learning and behavior problems were referred to our clinics by their teachers. Many of these children (15 percent of our total case load) were diagnosed as having an overly dependent personality disorder.[5] Such children were chronically helpless, clinging, and overdependent in their relationships with grownups. With other children their age they were inclined to be bossy, demanding, and fretful. Learning situations that demanded some autonomy, self-assertion, curiosity, and initiative were difficult for them. At times in the classroom or at home, to cover their anxiety at being asked to perform some task on their own, the children exhibited markedly controlling and demanding behavior. At these times infantile temper tantrums were common. Frustrated parents and teachers often described these children as "big babies" or as "immature." At other times they covered their anxieties by appearing to conform to home and school demands, but they continually provoked adults or other children by their negativism, stubbornness, dawdling, procrastination, and other measures. When these oppositional tendencies invaded the learning process, learning difficulties arose from the children's patterns of blocking out, "failing to hear," or passively resisting the external authority of the teacher. Much of their negativism and clowning seemed designed to get individual attention; they seemed able to function autonomously only by employing such negative adaptive maneuvers.

These emotional disorders were characterized by chronic maladjustive trends that had become ingrained in the children's personality structure. The parents of these children, both in their current patterns and in the histories of their child-rearing practices, revealed themselves to be generally indulgent, overprotective, and infantilizing of their children. Most signs of self-assertion and autonomy in the children had been squelched at an early age. Presumably, this allowed the parents to retain complete domination and possession of the children with no threat from any degree of separated functioning.

These personality disorders were usually not seen in consistently occurring, structured trait form until the child had reached school age. The histories of development of these children revealed, however, that premonitory patterns like these disorders were present at a preschool age. Had the children been referred and diagnosed earlier, these premonitory patterns would in all probability have been called deviations in social development.

In these children with overly dependent personality disorders, decompensation in the face of external stress happened occasionally, with the appearance of some sort of neurotic symptom superimposed upon the basic personality picture. For example, one twelve-year-old girl with an overly dependent personality developed an acute school-phobic reaction when her family was thrown into further turmoil by her father's acute, severe illness. By the same token, many of the acute and chronic school-phobic children discussed earlier had underlying overly dependent personalities.

Cynthia, a seven-year-old first grader, was an only child. In early interviews with me she often pouted, talked like a baby, and sucked her finger. She was referred by her teacher for procrastination, dawdling, and overbabyish ways, and by her family physician for her excessive fearfulness. Her father, a sawmill employee, had been off work for several months because of an injury. As Cynthia put it: "That buzz saw just grabbed daddy and bit his arm! The next time it'll eat him up! Mommy says so." Currently the child was frightened of rainstorms, thunder, the sound of her mother's pressure cooker during canning, pork frying, and a variety of other loud or sudden noises. In the one-room schoolhouse she attended, Cynthia was clinging, demanding, falling behind in her work, and preoccupied with fantasies of further injury to her family while she was gone. For years her parents "petted on" her—a term used by one of their neighbors to describe the family's relationships. Always a restless sleeper from birth, Cynthia had never slept apart from her mother. Both parents forbade her to visit neighbor children in the hollow. They feared she would be injured on the road. Her mother bathed her, dressed and undressed her, cut up her meat, and tied her shoes. Both parents spoke of Cynthia fondly as "our baby."

Eddie, a boy of eight, also related and talked in interviews like a much younger child. He was referred by his teacher at the beginning of the school year during which he was repeating first grade. The year before, Eddie had accomplished little in the classroom. He sat passively, seemed preoccupied, and learned little. His classmates teased him repeatedly as a "crybaby" and "sissy." Eddie lived at home with his father, a hardworking farmer of eighty acres, and his older sister, a high school senior. The father and Eddie together still mourned the death of their wife and mother two years before from cancer. Father and son had been close for years even before her death. But her passing drew them even closer. They slept together. Eddie was dressed, undressed, and bathed by his father. Neither allowed the other out of his sight on the farm. Neighbors thought of the father as a maternal man, who "petted on" Eddie. The father, a deacon in a small country church, spent his weekends exhorting the congregation to a pure family life, visiting the sick, and singing at funerals. Eddie always accompanied his father on these visits.

DEVIATIONS IN SOCIAL DEVELOPMENT

This subgroup of emotional disorders in preschool children involves deviations in some aspect of social relationships which are beyond the range of normal variation. The several preschool boys and girls we followed in this group exhibited delayed or uneven patterns of social capacities and relationships with others.[6] However, these problems had not yet crystallized into true personality disorders. These young children (5 percent of our total case load) were described by the family physicians and nurses who referred them as "too tied to Mother's apron strings." Although they had not yet developed overly dependent personality disorders, the trend of training at home was in this direction.

These children, whom we categorized as having deviations in social development, exhibited delayed achievement of autonomy (in the capacity for separation from their parents), marked shyness, overdependence on others, inhibitions, and immaturely aggressive behavior. They were particularly anxious on occasions demanding separation from their parents, such as a visit to the dentist or physician or beginning in a Head Start program. At these times they were whining and demanding, or shy and withdrawn, always clinging, and they had frequent temper tantrums. Their parents were generally infantilizing, hovering, and overprotective. In these respects, they were like the parents of older children having overly dependent personalities. Many of the parents—especially the mothers—had been overly close with their own parents. The illness of a family member and financial pressures were the two most prominent current reinforcers of the mother's already established need to maintain overclose ties with her child. The fathers were often quite aware of the mother's binding the child to her but seemed passive and peripheral; they were unable to support their wives or to help alter the alliance. Though some fathers were frustrated and even angry at their wives' inability to allow the children to separate, they were unable to do anything about it before clinic treatment discussions were begun. But then most of these fathers became powerful allies of both the treatment team and their families in redirecting the children's development along more autonomous lines.

We have found families of these preschool children to be quite amenable to psychological treatment by public health nurses and nursing students. The nurses generally saw a family in the home environment—mother, father, and child together. The family, onstage in its most natural setting, provided the nurse a clear view of the many obvious or even subtle ways in which the child was being trained in closeness. The nurse could, on the spot, mirror these relationships and inappropriate training techniques to the parents. The family was then helped to behave more appropriately in those situations in which the child gave a clear indication that he wanted to function more independently. We found that the nurse was in the best position, in the home setting with all family members present, to clarify the parents' training approaches, to explore underlying separation anxieties with the parents, and to suggest redirection of effort. We thought of home treatment of this type as reeducational in a developmental sense. In responding well to a half-dozen or more of these treatment visits, most of these families followed a pattern consistent with experience others have had nationally with children with similar early, nonfixed developmental problems. Our follow-up experience indicated these treated families did quite well. Most of the children adjusted better to separations, as in beginning first grade later on, for example. The passage of time, the process of working through provided by minimal help from the nurses, and the families' inherent potential for redirected development had led to correction of a large majority of these preschool disorders.

In a few instances, apparently when a particular family was unable to change its training patterns, the child's early problem continued. Follow-up of several of these latter, still-immature children indicated that they developed later a more structured overly dependent personality disorder. Our experience has been that, even with prolonged psychological treatment of the child and his family, fixed personality disorders of this overly dependent type are very difficult to modify, if in fact they can be changed at all. The best we achieved in such cases was an amelioration to some extent of the binding forces interacting in the family, with a resultant mild-to-moderate improvement in the children's abilities to separate and to learn. Though we viewed these results as gains sufficient to warrant time spent with these families, they stand in sharp contrast with the excellent results obtained by early intervention with families with preschool children. For best results, overclose families should be referred when their child is young. As one of our trainees put it: "I feel with a preschooler like this I'm dealing with an acorn, before he gets to be a bent oak tree!" Certainly, our data on treatment of both the older children with overly dependent personality disorders and the preschool children with deviations in social development suggest a real need for early case-finding on a local or perhaps regional level. A regional pediatric clinic, for example, would seem to be a logical place in which to begin this search.

Our data further indicate the great effectiveness of public health nurses as local treatment personnel for the less troubled, nonfixed early cases. With family physicians so scarce and overworked in Eastern Kentucky, as in the wider Southern Appalachian region, this fact has important implications for mental health manpower planning. The following family example illustrates the clinical features of a deviation in social development in their preschool child and underscores the effective treatment results obtained by the family and the public health nurse who worked with them.

Charlie, a sturdy three-year-old boy with teddy-bear appeal, was referred to the clinic by his family physician. At times, during routine physical examinations, Charlie had been unusually fearful of separating from his mother and also of procedures. Apparent, too, was the mother's infantilizing and overprotection of the boy.

Following the physician's referral, the public health nurse met for several visits with Charlie's parents and the boy, their only child, in the family's small trailer home. Family roles and patterns of relating were clear. The nurse perceived that the family, like a frightened turtle, had confined much of their world to the shell-like trailer.

George, Charlie's father, a handsome but cautious young man of twenty-four, was at that time recovering gradually from a severe depressive illness. He was maintaining his small family on public-assistance funds while preparing to become an auto mechanic at a nearby vocational school. Eula, Charlie's mother, was twenty-two. She was an inhibited, dependent person and attempted to lean heavily on her husband. His own personality and illness prevented him from providing much emotional support to his wife. Consequently, Eula turned to her young son in an attempt to have her needs met, and became wrapped up in his care. During the initial visits, the nurse saw Eula fully dress Charlie and feed him herself. Charlie's rare attempts to play in the fenced yard around the trailer mobilized his mother's separation concerns. She warned him of potential death on the distant highway beyond the fence and of the dangers inherent in his tricycle. Charlie's real attempts at times to help himself or to play alone turned into regressive pleas that his mother do it for him or accompany him.

The nurse became the family's therapist in the home, making herself available to them several times each week. Over the following four months significant progress was made. Eula was receptive to the nurse as a source of dependent support and later accepted her as a demonstrator of more appropriate ways of relating to Charlie. George responded favorably to the interest taken in his wife, son, and home by the nurse by beginning to show interest of his own. His wife's positive reception of his reawakened interest, and the nurse's further support, encouraged him to complete his schooling and to initiate plans for a later job. He began to spend some time with Charlie, relating increasingly well with his son and helping him acquire age-appropriate skills.

Following this more active period of treatment, the nurse began gradually to limit her contacts. Previously established gains held. The nurse had periodic supportive contacts with the family until after Charlie had entered school and his father was well established in his job.

SYMBIOTIC PSYCHOSIS

For six years we evaluated and followed three children with symbiotic psychosis (the comparative rarity of this severe emotional disorder in our large clinic group is nonetheless greater than the crude incidence data available for the nation). One of these children, Tony, merits attention here because his problem sharply highlights the regional emphasis on family closeness. His psychopathology, in one sense, represents an exaggerated form of the regional symbiosis apparent in a remarkable number of parent-child relationships.

As formulated nationally,[7] symbiotic psychosis involves children who seem to have developed reasonably adequately for the first year or two of life, with awareness of and an attachment to the mother appearing during the first year. Subsequently the child may show unusual dependence upon the mother in the form of an intensification and prolongation of the attachment. He apparently fails to master the next developmental step—separation and individuation. In the second to fourth or fifth year, the onset of the psychotic disorder occurs, ordinarily in relation to some real or fantasied threat to the mother-child relationship. The child, often suddenly, shows intense separation anxiety and clinging. This appears together with regressive manifestations, the later frequently including the giving up of communicative speech. The child may then be mute, or he may utter only jargon words or sounds imitative of noises in the immediate world about him. He usually exhibits gradual withdrawal and emotional aloofness, eventually leading to an intense desire to be left completely alone. He may show an intense desire for the same few material possessions he retreats to in private play to the exclusion of relating with others. If others intrude into his private play and reverie, he reacts with frenzied panic. Or he may become similarly disorganized through panic if the symbiotic partner, usually the mother, leaves or threatens to leave him. Overall, he seems silently locked in to a very private experiential world with a few things but without people, except for his mother. Jiggle this private world, and panic ensues.

Tony, who was otherwise a perfectly healthy youngster, was the child who painfully lived out these kinds of emotional troubles. He was referred to the mental health clinic by his parents at age seven. The family had a modest but adequate income from a small bottomland farm. Although Tony's mother was a chronically tense, perfectionistic person, she had until the time of the boy's birth related well with her three daughters, provided a neat and attractive home, and maintained a duty-oriented marriage. Her personal background involved bonds of obligation and duty, little affection, a religious view of poverty and recurrent disease as God's will, and belief in the dictum that things should be accepted as they are—and in silence. As a child, furthermore, she agonized each time her own mother bemoaned the deaths of her three older brothers, each of whom had died a traumatic death before the age of nine.

After Tony was born, his mother changed remarkably. She became tense, obsessed with the idea that her healthy infant son would fall ill or would die accidentally. Gradually she withdrew from her husband and daughters and devoted herself to warding off unseen dangers that might harm Tony. She and Tony were inseparable. At the age of three, Tony spoke only single meaningful words, and only to his mother. After receiving a large burn on his chest, he slept with her every night. He seemed almost unaware that his father and sisters existed, and he rarely spoke near them. His face was wooden, almost constantly expressionless, except during those times of panic when his mother was absent for a moment. Uninvolved with peers, siblings, and his father, Tony spent his days playing out highly intricate tableaux with toys near his mother.

During evaluation we came to feel that Tony was not mentally retarded, because of his general hyperalertness to stimuli, his amazingly intricate play performances, and the considerable detail of his spontaneous drawings. A generally healthy boy, he was found to have no neuromuscular or neurological problems. The striking moment during evaluation came when Tony was separated from his mother. He rushed in a headlong frenzy through every room and corridor of the health department. As he fled, he wet and soiled himself and uttered broken, jargon sounds and outcries. During his flight he stumbled onto a clerk-typist, a woman his mother's age and quite like her in appearance. Into this woman's lap Tony crawled, attempting almost to melt into her with his embrace. His mother at this time was equally irrationally frightened.

At the present time, Tony is completing fairly successfully a three-year period of residential hospital treatment. He will rejoin his family, themselves improved, as a differentiated, much less symbiotic child.

PSYCHOPHYSIOLOGIC DISORDERS

Children of all ages were frequently referred to our local clinics with various psychophysiologic (psychosomatic) disorders. Such disorders have also been diagnosed in large numbers of children from Eastern Kentucky whose family physicians have referred them to the University of Kentucky Medical Center in Lexington since its opening in 1962. Though our field data and the University hospital data do not yield epidemiologically valid prevalence rates for these disorders, the combined data do strongly suggest that psychophysiologic disorders in children constitute a major mental health problem among the people of Eastern Kentucky. Evidence indicates that the pattern continues in adults in the region.[8]

The psychophysiologic disorders most frequently encountered in preschool and younger school-age children were severe loss of appetite for a period, psychogenic vomiting, enuresis (wetting), recurrent abdominal pain, recurrent headache, and syncopal attacks (fainting spells). Older school-age children and adolescents had peptic ulcers, encopresis (fecal soiling), asthma, eczema, and ulcerative colitis (bleeding from the large bowel), as well as the disorders listed for the younger age group. Vomiting, headache, fainting, and enuresis were the most common; sometimes an individual child had several of these problems at the same time.

As defined nationally,[9] psychophysiologic disorders are illnesses involving dysfunctions of the autonomic nervous system and visceral organs which are in part or even largely (usually not wholly) the result of chronic emotional stress. The group is subclassified according to the organ system affected and the specific symptoms. The causative influences leading to the development of psychophysiologic disorders are only partially known. These illnesses can generally be looked upon as the body's maladaptations to situations that have been the source of chronic emotional stress.

Why chronic emotional stress causes some individuals to develop physical disorders instead of purely emotional disorders, and why one such individual suffers dysfunction of one organ system or organ instead of another, are not well understood. Genetic inheritance may well play an important role in the etiology of some psychophysiologic disorders, although very little is known about this. At the present, partial state of our understanding, psychophysiologic disorders are regarded simply as the outcome of a complexity of influences both within and outside the individual. One must consider the factors within the individual himself—his unique genetic inheritance, his environmental experiences, and the level of maturation he has attained—and the situation which is acutely, or chronically, emotionally stressful for him and with which he is attempting to cope.[10]

In connection with these disorders, it is interesting to note that the expression of emotional stress in infancy—the preverbal stage of human development—is always visceral and motor. Babies don't talk about their discomfort, they flush, belch, and squirm about. Some writers feel that these normal bodily manifestations of stress may in some individuals be overused or exaggerated and thereby may be the precursors of later psychophysiologic disorders. To quote Emanuel Miller: "We ought, in studying the emotional disturbances of children which are precursors of somatic disorders, to make observations that will establish *primary situations which create a sort of central autonomic disposition* on which all future expressions, mental as well as somatic, will depend, or to which they may regress in times of stress."[11]

Our work with children with psychophysiologic disorders in

Eastern Kentucky has yielded two themes that excite us with respect to Miller's suggestion that we seek to learn if there are "primary situations which create a sort of . . . disposition [to such disorders]." The first theme, which has already received prominent mention, is the emphasis on early training in family closeness, found in perhaps a majority of Eastern Kentucky families but carried to a pathologic degree in some. In the families of children with psychophysiologic disorders, we consistently saw demonstrations of overcloseness, with accompanying signs that conflicts related to separation were sources of continual tension in the family. The second theme, interwoven with the first, is that children with psychophysiologic disorders, and their parents as well, were significantly nonverbal compared with children who either had no emotional problems or had emotional problems of another sort.

Consequences of Early Training in Closeness

Review of the personalities and living circumstances of these children indicated that acute episodes of psychophysiologic disorders were consistently precipitated by conflicts involving intense separation anxiety. Many of the children had overly dependent personalities. They related with their parents and others in a chronically helpless, clinging, and dependent manner. Tasks demanding autonomy and initiative were difficult for them. They showed markedly controlling and demanding behavior. Parents of these children, both in how they related now with their children and in histories of how they raised them, were generally indulgent, overprotective, and infantilizing.

By contrast with this infantilized subgroup, several other children had overly independent personalities, with tendencies toward overly responsible behavior. In attempting to act beyond their years they tended to deny feelings of underlying separation anxiety, feelings of helplessness, or dependent needs. Parents of these children were generally tense, compulsive, and denying of their own separation anxiety. They had a need to push their children toward too-early independence. Many of the families of the children with psychophysiologic disorders overreacted to the illness of any member, illness frequently serving to focus mutual separation concerns.

Nonverbality

In contrast with other clinic families, those of the children with psychophysiologic disorders seemed particularly nonverbal.

In interviews all family members had considerable difficulty talking with 'one another. They had trouble expressing intense or conflicted feelings. It seemed especially hard for them to talk about their intense separation anxieties or, without considerable support, to discuss the events that had triggered off this anxiety. As these children and their parents sat relatively silently through the early interviews, there was ample nonverbal evidence that they were experiencing disturbing feelings. They frowned, twisted, blanched, and flushed, and occasionally they hyperventilated, felt dizzy, or vomited.

Later on, with much support, the children began to open up. Hesitantly at first, then sometimes in a torrent, words came forth. Many of them were poignant words, full of meaning, like these from a curly-haired six-year-old girl: "And when I go to school I lay my head down there on that desk, Buddy, and then I get sad 'cause Daddy gets drunk and he ain't got no license for that there old car and Mommy worries so when he drives the coal truck may come and smash him and I get this headache 'cross my eyes and pains in my stomach and then I puke, Buddy."

Many parents made attempts to silence such children: "Hush, Baby, don't fret. It's all right. We won't talk about it!" It was these parents our trainees thought might fit the old stereotype of the taciturn Eastern Kentuckian. Neighbors did characterize some of them in local argot as "quiet-turned." We worked with these family-closeness and nonverbal themes in the lives of the following children.

Kathy and Dora were nine-year-old identical twins from a poor family. Each developed psychogenic vomiting on occasions of separation from their parents—school entrance each fall, and the frequent hospitalization of both parents for a variety of chronic illnesses. Each child was clinging, helpless, demanding, and controlling of others. Their daydreams, drawings, and statements were filled with themes of separation concerns: "Daddy's got the heart trouble and he sneaks medicine but we know he takes it. He says he's all right, but Mommy cries and gets sick and goes to the hospital for her woman trouble. Will they die?"

Psychological testing showed that both girls were of above-average intelligence. Projective-test protocols indicated that each child assumed an invalid role, avoided the kind of assertive behavior characteristic of her age, and preferred to lean on others for support and direction. Parents denied, repressed, and uged suppression of all feelings, particularly separation anxiety. In relative silence the family clung in interdependence through a succession of actual disasters (floods, fires, illnesses) and anticipated disasters.

Linda, age fifteen, was from a middle-class farm family. Since early infancy, she had had waxing and waning chronic eczema in the creased areas of her skin. Her personality involved marked behavioral and verbal inhibition, chronic and excessive concern with conformity, and some negativism and other oppositional features. She had an extremely negative self-concept, with strong feelings of inferiority and inadequacy, accompanied by some depression. She dramatized this by comparing herself with the central figure in Kentucky writer Jesse Stuart's book *God's Oddling*.[12] Oversensitive and self-critical, she felt ineffective and under the control of adults. Even though she was easily hurt by criticism, felt deprived of satisfactions in life, and was dejected and discouraged, on the surface there was a Pollyanna-like denial and evasion of troubles outside of her bodily complaints.

Interview and projective-test evidence suggested that these attitudes stemmed from a long-standing disturbance in Linda's relationship with her mother. She experienced her mother (whose personality was very similar to Linda's) consciously and unconsciously as overprotective and rejecting. Her father was experienced as passive, peripheral, and silent. Linda's unresolved conflicts revolved around chronic hostility, related to her frustrated dependency longings, and anxiety and guilt over related separation themes. In each new stressful situation (leaving home to attend a summer church camp, a financial crisis in the family) she could not voice her conflicted feelings but experienced further redness and weeping of her skin.

In crisis situations like Linda's and Kathy's and Dora's, our treatment goal was to aid the children and their parents to express previously blocked feelings. This often served to eliminate, or to reduce the severity of, psychophysiologic disorders in the children, and it also reduced family tensions. Such therapeutic effort, of course, did not alter the underlying personality traits of the children. Nor did success with this type of crisis intervention guarantee that the individual family would continue to express feelings verbally in the future. Many of the families were lost to longer-term interview therapy because, like many action-oriented families, they expected and welcomed help only in the symptomatic, crisis situation.

Comparisons

The nonverbal observations we made on these families parallel the formulations of Thomas Szasz and Edwin Weinstein. Both of these researchers conceptualize the central theme in psychosomatic medicine as follows: Previously nonverbalized conflicted feelings are expressed in various forms of bodily illness as a type of body language. Szasz has stated: "As a rule, the use of this type of body language is fostered by circumstances which make direct verbal expression difficult or impossible."[13] Weinstein finds that the clinical nonverbal observations we have made are very close to his own comparisons, and he indicates that in psychosomatic research these verval/nonverbal comparisons have not been studied generally.[14]

Our clinical data suggest the hypothesis, I feel, that blocked verbal expression is only one factor in the subsequent expression of conflicted feelings in the body-language form we call a psychophysiologic disorder. A second factor, which seems just as essential in producing a psychophysiologic disorder, is the current focal and the underlying developmental, or training, conflicts. In these Eastern Kentucky children with psychophysiologic disorders, the prominent focal conflicts were those involving separation anxiety. The developmental conflicts involved a prolongation of an infantile-dependent adjustment in the child. Therefore, I feel our data suggest that specific, unresolved infantile-dependent conflicts and blocked verbal expression of feelings operate together, or constitute the two necessary causative factors, in the development of psychophysiologic disorders in these children.

ABSENT DISORDERS

Most striking to us as we worked with Eastern Kentucky families over the six-year period was the absence of two severe emotional disorders in children. One is early infantile autism, or autistic psychosis of early childhood. The other is the severe personality disorder in children termed a primary behavior disorder.[15] Both of these disorders are generally considered to be based either wholly or in large part on extreme emotional deprivation of children in their infancy. Both essentially involve a lack of basic relatedness. The roots of relatedness for all children are considered by most child developmentalists to begin in infancy in the mother-child relationship. As Erik Erikson describes it, a child learns to love his mother and to develop from their relationship an abiding sense of basic trust that generalizes to all future relationships.[16] It is, in Erikson's opinion, this basic trust in others that forms the keystone of all relatedness.

Early Infantile Autism

Early infantile autism appears to have its onset during the first few months or the first year of life, with the infant failing to develop an attachment to the mother. He remains aloof, showing little awareness of human contact, and is preoccupied with inanimate objects. The development of speech is delayed or absent; when it does appear, speech is not employed appropriately, for purposes of communication. The child shows a strong need to maintain sameness; he resists change, responding with marked outbursts of temper or acute and intense anxiety when routines are altered. Sleeping and feeding habits are often bizarre. Motor patterns are often stereotyped and primitive. There is no pattern to intellectual development; it may be normal, possibly advanced, or it may be restricted and uneven in areas. In any case, the lack of the capacity to perceive reality correctly and to communicate through speech may render most intellectual functions ineffective.[17]

Parents of such children are described frequently as unable to relate with their infants. They remain cold, withdrawn, aloof, mechanistic. Leo Kanner called them "refrigerator parents." My own experience with parents of autistic children in the urban settings of Baltimore, Cincinnati, and Lexington over the past twelve years parallels Kanner's observations.

Primary Behavior Disorders

These children show extremely shallow relationships with adults or other children. They have very low frustration tolerance. They exhibit great difficulty in controlling their impulses, both sexual and aggressive, which are discharged immediately and impulsively, without delay or inhibition and often without any regard for the consequences. Little anxiety, internalized conflict, or guilt is experienced by most of these children, because the conflict remains largely external, between society and their impulses.

The basic defects in relatedness and impulse controls appear to be reinforced by a deficit in conscience. These children fail to develop the capacity to store tension and to postpone gratifications. They ordinarily exhibit primitive coping mechanisms, with strong denial of dependent or other needs, projection of their hostile feelings onto adults or society, and rationalization of their own behavior.[18]

Such children often have a history of extreme emotional deprivation during infancy and early childhood, marked by frequent and prolonged separations from mothering figures. In a sense, they grow up unloved, unwanted, and rejected. They feel unlovable, and they behave in ways consistent with their low self-regard—stealing, fire setting, vandalism, aggressive attack, and other antisocial acts. A large number of such children have been reported from lower socioeconomic or social class groups in urban settings.[19]

Speculation

During the six-year period of our fieldwork in Eastern Kentucky with over nine hundred families (287 clinic families; 650 children reviewed in school consultation) no cases of early infantile autism or primary behavior disorder were encountered. During the same period three autistic children and five with primary behavior disorders were reviewed in the Child Psychiatry Clinic, Department of Psychiatry, University of Kentucky Medical Center in Lexington. These severely disturbed children were from essentially urban, Central Kentucky families, and from all three major socioeconomic classes. The Child Psychiatry Clinic total case load during that period was approximately 250 children. These incidence figures, though admittedly crude, roughly parallel my previous experience with severely disturbed children in child psychiatry clinics in urban settings, at the University of Maryland Psychiatric Institute in Baltimore and at the University of Cincinnati College of Medicine.

It should be recalled that our field data on children in Eastern Kentucky are not epidemiological data: we do not have true prevalence rates for each emotional disorder we encountered. But for these rural counties our data roughly approximate prevalence figures, we feel, because of the thorough knowledge each public health nurse has of all the families in her district case load. Though it may have been possible for a nurse to overlook such a severely disturbed child in her district, that seems quite unlikely.

The absence of these two severe emotional disorders in Eastern Kentucky children merits attention. I raise the hypothesis that the regional training focus on infants precludes the formation of these severe disturbances, which are based on extreme emotional deprivation in infancy. No Eastern Kentucky family emotionally deprives an infant or young child. If anything, these families overgive to infants.

DERIVATIVE STRENGTHS

We have come to view the regional family training focus on infancy as a two-edged sword. Pathological exaggeration of this developmental focus occurs in some families and can frequently lead to emotional problems in children. That is one cutting edge of the sword. The other edge, which is presumably a result of the normal-level regional focus on infancy, is a derivative strength possessed by a majority of Eastern Kentucky adults and children. This strength (some would call it one part of a person's ego functioning) is a marked capacity for essentially trusting relatedness. Although the adults and children we have met, in and out of the clinics, may be initially shy and reserved, showing some suspiciousness toward outsiders, they soon drop this initial guardedness and relate in very personal, often intense ways. A trainee described this capacity: "Once these kids thaw out, they relate better with me than the ones I see back home!"

Theoretical Background

One of the most important developmental tasks of the infant during the first year is to establish a satisfying dependency upon his mother. The mother-child relationship can be a close, satisfying, and supportive one. The previous work of other observers and our own survey on Eastern Kentucky child development suggest how abundantly true this is for local infants. Although in the years to follow Eastern Kentucky children encounter difficulties in development—particularly children of the lower class—that first year or two of infancy is, from the infant's standpoint, relatively conflict-free.

Out of the mother-child relationship comes the foundation for the development of the child's feelings about himself, about people, and about the world in which he lives. If the relationship is a satisfying one, the infant begins to develop a sense of trust in himself and in his world, the first year being the decisive stage for the acquisition of this feeling.[20] He acquires a feeling of his own worth and adequacy and a feeling that the world is a pleasant, giving, and rewarding place. He begins to feel that people can be trusted. He is interested in the world. He investigates, explores, and tests. He attempts to communicate and to make meaningful interpersonal relationships. Relatedness is very much a positive derivative of an adequate infancy.

Eastern Kentucky Relatedness

Our first impression of the inherently strong capacity Eastern Kentucky families of all three social classes have for trusting relationships was gained from their children. They related very well in clinic interviews, in their schools at the time of our consultation visits, and in their homes. Any initial reserve was soon dropped. Their capacity to relate led them to wait quietly, even with nonanxious anticipation, for their dental appointments in the health departments and for preschool physical examinations by strange visiting pediatricians. Most of us as urban physicians are accustomed to the waiting-room crying and restlessness of young children. Thus I was at first surprised to find Eastern Kentucky children waiting quietly, without crying, or excitedly giggling with each other. A passing adult could quickly relate with a waiting child and find pleasure in their encounter.

The Eastern Kentucky child's capacity to form a quick, trusting relationship with the public health nurses and our medical team was a prime mover in the rapid progress many children made in treatment interviews. Success in nursing intervention, casework, and psychotherapy, wherever it is practiced, depends on the relationship between therapist and child. It is the touchstone of any progress out of whatever difficulties the child may have.

The same could equally be said of the parents of these children: adults, too, related well with others, although the thawing-out period was sometimes longer than the time required by the children. Once their initial reticence was overcome, however, parents made good use of the relationship aspects of treatment. In time, they were able to involve themselves in interviews with remarkable warmth and candor. Although many families were geographically and culturally outside the mainstream of county life, they related with us generally with no sense of personal isolation. In fact, their relatedness often combined such warmth, openness, and earthiness that we were reminded of the traditional spontaneity of young children. Gone were the layers of sophistication—telling the physician and others what families think should be said—that so often marks, and impedes, initial treatment interviews with urban families. Such qualities of relatedness enabled the therapist to focus very quickly on family functioning.

Because so many of the families referred to the mental health clinics were action oriented, seeking primarily symptomatic relief for crisis situations, the mutual capacity for relationship of therapist and parents had to be quickly utilized as the basis for helping a given family redirect its efforts with the children. Parents more readily tried out redirective suggestions made by the therapist because they had quickly established a bond with this outside person.

Of great interest to us as clinicians was the observation that the basic capacity for relatedness seemed to cross socioeconomic class lines. For example, the often grubby, ragged children of the lower class we saw were frequently wild, impulse ridden, and manipulative. But along with these traits was a warm way of reaching out to others that we interpreted as essential relatedness. Although in time we saw many lower-class children who related well, I shall always remember the unique reaching-out of John Henry, the first boy referred to us from this group.

Seven years old, John Henry was a middle child of eight. The family lived in a two-room cabin up at the end of a dry-creek road, isolated from other families in the hollow. Squalor marked every aspect of their lives. The parents were out of work, grim, and resigned. They were completely unable to relate to, or set any limits for, the older children, who ran wild.

The school in the district initially directed our attention to John Henry, who seldom attended. The public health nurse had difficulty making contact with the family to set up a health department clinic appointment. They fled from her jeep and shut themselves into the cabin. When the parents had finally been persuaded to come to the clinic, the caseworker deduced that they were completely unable to cope with their older children. They smiled only in response to questions about their infants and indicated they felt able to take some care of them.

My initial interview with John Henry was chaotic. The boy was wild, impulsive, and constantly asked me for cigarettes. But through his grime and rags his face shone with delight as he related with me. He was never withdrawn or suspicious when alone with me, established eye-contact readily, and seemed to want to be near me. In spite of all the chaos, John Henry related well.

Sometimes these two personality traits—being able to relate well and being aggressively, wildly impulsive—found extraordinary expression in several generations of members of the same lower-class family. The Hawkins family was like this. They had a colorful reputation in their county of being the hardest-drinking, hardest-fighting, and yet most intensely loyal, good-natured bunch around. Kinship ties were extremely strong among them. A referral to us of thirteen-year-old George, a Hawkins boy, came in the wake of aggressive acting-out by George himself and by his guardian aunt Lettie.

When we first saw Lettie and George, in the waiting room of the local health department, they made quite a pair. The aunt, a short, stocky, weathered woman wearing a clean, faded cotton dress, a broad-brimmed cotton hat, and short boots, was the picture of aroused militancy. She sat there ramrod straight, pinning George down beside her with an unwavering glare. He, a muscular, dark, brooding boy, seemed to share her mood. As Lettie sat and chewed her front lip and glared at George, he glowered back at her unflinchingly. I had the initial impression, as the caseworker and I came up with their nurse to meet them, that one word from any one of us might set off a battle between these two.

As we approached, Lettie, still fixing George with her glare, began complaining of his "doin's and car'in'-ons" in a very loud, husky voice. "Ever since this hyar young-un came to live with me hit's been trouble. He's been lickin' all the others [George, it turned out, had five younger brothers and sisters], stompin' through the house and yellin' at me like he's got all outdoors to do hit in! Hit's a sight to make him mind. I got more blisters on my hands than he's got on his behind from that there board I use with him. But hit ain't no use. He's born black and trouble!" Oddly enough, Lettie's bristling recital of George's sins had a matter-of-fact sort of feeling to it; it was delivered almost with a sense of pride. What was missing from her statement was a feeling of much anger. George seemed to sense this. As Lettie thundered on, he alternately grinned and glowered back at her. This rather curious mixture of pride, pleasure, and mutual aggressive glaring at each other was subsequently traced back in their histories.

George and his brothers and sisters had come to live with

their paternal aunt Lettie, a widow, in her house eight months before the time we first saw them. The children had moved in with her because they had lost both of their parents quite suddenly: Lettie herself had shot them one evening. The story went that the couple, both of whom, like all the Hawkinses, were wild and given to impulsive spree drinking, had crawled up onto Lettie's cabin porch that evening "drunkener than a lord," yelled at Lettie (it was apparently just one more episode in a long-standing family quarrel), and threatened her with harm. Lettie came out with her shotgun—as she told the jury later—and killed her younger brother and sister-in-law "fer molestin'." She was acquitted, on the grounds of self-defense. "Hawkinses are just that way with each other," was a phrase we heard over and over from others in that particular community. However, no one could recall any time that a Hawkins had ever seriously injured anyone or committed a crime against the personal property of anyone, other than an immediate family member. Apparently, even their wild, impulsive, aggressive acts followed kinship lines quite closely. Whatever they did, the Hawkinses did together.

Beneath her gruff, aggressive exterior Lettie revealed herself to be a warm, personable woman whom I liked a great deal immediately. She had none of those cold, distance-promoting, detached qualities that usually mark the relationships of the urban dissocial or antisocial people who shoot others. Here, instead, was a friendly, trusting, warm, loud, wild woman.

She told us that day at the clinic that it was her "bounden duty" to take over the care of George and the other children after their parents' deaths. She had no complaints about the others. After the funerals they had "settled in fine! They's stopped snivelin', mind, and get their lessons." But George, in Lettie's judgment, was "another one, cuss him! He's got a chip on him, gets riled easy-like jus' like his Daddy and all us Hawkinses do." It was with mingled complaint and pride that Lettie told us George was very much like both his father and herself. Her pride in George, which the boy sensed deeply, actually outweighed her concerns about him. The referral to us bore out her feelings. It had been George's fifth-grade teacher, who sensed the boy was depressed underneath his flippant, chip-on-the-shoulder, I-need-nothing-from-nobody attitude at school, who referred the two of them to us.

The teacher was right; George was mildly depressed following the loss of his parents. More remarkable, however, was his close, warm attachment to his aunt Lettie and his great pride in her, which—as she did reciprocally—he attempted to conceal under a crusty veneer of shouting, yelling, constant complaining, and misbehaving. He consciously forgave his aunt for shooting his parents: "Damn fools had it comin' to 'em!" At a deeper level, outside his awareness much of the time, he reacted to the loss with feelings of sadness. George's tie with his aunt actually prevented his depression from deepening. His underlying sadness lifted rather quickly as our talks together at the health department continued over the next four months. But over this period of time neither George nor Lettie changed the characteristic life-style: both continued to be personable, well-related, yet impulsively aggressive persons toward each other, and toward others.

Our conclusion from reviewing the developmental backgrounds of George, John Henry, and other children like them from the lower class in Eastern Kentucky was that these children are well trained in basic relatedness from infancy on, but are not trained well in acquiring controls over their aggressive impulses. The children are well liked as babies and as older children, but in many areas they are allowed to do just as they please. Beyond the children's infancy, appropriate developmental lines involving a balance between gratification of needs and delays, limits, and controls are not readily maintained by lower-class families in Eastern Kentucky. This seemed to account for the difficulties older lower-class children had with perceptual skills needed for orienting to a new environment, with communication skills, and with capacities to delay gratification and to establish internal impulse controls. But during the infancy period itself, lower-class families as well as the others freely gave of themselves to their children. As an outgrowth of this, the children retained a considerable measure of the ability to relate with others in spite of difficulties with other capacities.

The implications for the mental health field of this capacity for relatedness should not be underestimated. All forms of mental health intervention (treatment) involve the giving and the taking of help in an interpersonal context. In my experience, and that of others, the relationship capacities of Eastern Kentucky families are very real indeed, and these capacities are not dimmed by the families' migration to other settings. Presumably, then, those who work in any helping capacity with Eastern

Kentucky families, either locally or in another setting, will find mutual relationship a powerful working tool and thrust. When Weller and others[21] refer to "personalization of services," they are talking primarily about this capacity for relatedness. After relationships are established, services can then be brought into focus. One clinic parent put it graphically: "I like Mrs. Morelock and what she has to say—she's one of us!"

CHAPTER 5   In the Clinic:
                 Psychosexual
                 Themes

As has been abundantly indicated,
marked inner-directedness characterized a great majority of the families
that came to our clinics. Close, interdependent functioning was prominent
as well in those families reviewed in
our survey of Eastern Kentucky child
development. The training climate
for infants involved extremely close
ties with older family members. As
the children grew, closeness became
a training end in itself. Children were
taught in a myriad of verbal and nonverbal ways to maintain the close
family system. Events and situations
apparently viewed by parents as
potentially threatening to the closeness of the family were coped with
in a variety of ways. The toddler's
wandering off independently, for example, was usually handled by a
mixture of denial of his growing
autonomy ("out of sight, out of mind")
and relating to him in infantile ways
when he wandered back.

As these children grew into their
later preschool years, a crucial developmental task of this childhood
period seemed similarly threatening

to parents, namely, early infantile sexuality. Parents who spoke volubly about raising their children as infants became strikingly silent as I inquired about the usual developmental phenomena in their preschoolers: masturbation, sexual curiosity, genital exhibitionism, mutual sex play, and related sex-role games of mothers-and-fathers. The parents usually denied any knowledge that their four- and five-year-olds "did such things." But their blushing, stammering, and general discomfort betrayed their concern with these phenomena and with this aspect of preschool development as a whole.

This discomfort was not seen in most of the preschool children themselves, however. When their parents fell into embarrassed silence over a sexual turn in our interviews, preschoolers often began to drift closer to me with wide-eyed sidelong glances. I recall one family in particular. The mother and I had been talking comfortably in the living room, while an infant boy of one sat and played at our feet. During this time a girl of five and a boy of four had been chorusing over peanut butter and crackers in the kitchen, well within earshot. When my questions turned to sexual matters, the mother colored and fell silent. At that point the children came in from the kitchen, giving every indication they knew what I was talking about. The girl began to tell me how she and her younger brother played mothers-and-fathers with some old dishes out back by the smokehouse. But Mother interrupted: "Baby, Doctor doesn't want to hear about such things. Go and eat, now!" I was made to feel that I had violated a taboo.

That is precisely the point here. Sexual development, maturation, and functioning were difficult for most of our families to deal with, whether they were talking with their children or discussing these tasks with others. My speculation is that, for several reasons, sexual matters are troublesome for perhaps a majority of Eastern Kentucky families. First, there is the strong religious downgrading of sexuality long known to those who have reviewed life and culture in the Southern Appalachian region and in the wider region of the rural South—the Bible Belt. Although churches on the whole do not exert a strong social influence in Eastern Kentucky, religious taboos and restrictions do. Sexuality is still viewed as base, or sinful.

Second, this strongly accepted religious view of sexuality contrasts sharply with the facts of sexual maturation and functioning within the family itself. Preschoolers at first are doing what comes as naturally for them as for children anywhere else. In addition, the cramped living conditions of so many families throw a sharp light on anyone's sexuality. When large families sleep in one room, when two or more children sleep in one bed, there is little opportunity for modesty. The sexual intercourse of adults is often seen and heard. Accordingly, the sexual interest and activities of the children are likely to be overly stimulated. This clearly creates a conflict situation for most families. Religious views and sexual openness clash. The conflict, apparently an intense one, is resolved by the traditional coping techniques of Eastern Kentucky families. They turn inward, becoming silent in denial of the problem. This silence covers family members with one another as well as with an outside interviewer.

The public health nurses were well aware of this phenomenon. Although many women from the region wanted birth-control advice and the free contraceptive pills and devices available to them in their local health departments, they were slow in asking for this aid. Overcoming this reticence has taken time and patience. Examples of reluctance to discuss sexual matters are found everywhere in the region. Even now, many women are adamantly opposed to gynecological examinations by a male physician. In our school consultations we found teachers eager to discuss all kinds of problems in maladjusting children except sexual ones. This seemed to account in part for the difficulty the public health nurses encountered in starting sex-education courses in the local junior and senior high schools. The adults and adolescents followed in our clinics were rarely able to review their own sexual functioning with any degree of spontaneity. Unquestionably, sexuality was the most consistently difficult theme for clinic families to discuss.

We have thus found that older children and adolescents in the region have grown up in a training climate in which sexuality is to some extent regarded as inherently evil, one which says that sexuality in all forms should be avoided if possible—and if it cannot be avoided, at least it must not be talked about. The conflicts over sexual maturation and functioning cross socioeconomic class lines in Eastern Kentucky. But they seem strongest in lower-class families, for whom the open overcrowding forced upon them by poverty creates considerable sexual as well as other kinds of tensions.

Clearly related to this regional developmental theme of sexual conflict, we have felt from our clinical experience, is the frequent occurrence in children and adults of emotional disorders based primarily on such conflicts. From our work we have concluded that sexual conflicts were prominent in those adolescents with conversion reactions, in those adolescent girls with hysterical personality disorders, and in those adolescent boys with psychosexual identity problems. These conflicts also played a significant part in shaping the attitudes, feelings, and actions of many adults in the region.

CONVERSION REACTIONS

Clinical interest in grand hysteria, or hysterical reactions—as conversion reactions were formerly called—has existed for hundreds, even thousands of years. Hippocrates described the disorder as an affection of the mind caused primarily by a wandering uterus. Writers in the Middle Ages were familiar with the acute onset and the highly dramatic quality of the symptoms. In the last century Pierre Janet, Sigmund Freud, and Joseph Breuer devoted great clinical attention to hysteria. Freud, emphasizing the sexual conflicts prominent in the hysterical disorders of his adult women patients, felt that sexual symbolism was a basic feature of the various symptoms of these disorders. He believed that the Victorian conflict over sexual maturation and functioning accounted in part for the frequent occurrence of hysteria in European women.

In our own time, hysteria has more and more taken on a regional flavor. Though sporadic conversion reactions occur in middle- and upper-class urban American families, more cases can be found among lower- and working-class families in the Southern Appalachian region and the rural South as a whole. In addition, conversion reactions are frequently encountered among Appalachian migrants. James Proctor noted many conversion reactions in school-age children and adolescents in western North Carolina.[1] Weston LaBarre, a cultural anthropologist at Duke University, was interested in the on-the-spot conversion reactions frequently experienced by adolescent girls and young women attending snake-handling religious services, which are highly symbolic sexually.[2] LaBarre goes on to broaden this clinical view, taking careful note of the problems with sexual maturation and functioning shared by nearly all rural Southerners. He indicates that the rural South retains a severely ascetic Protestant ethos regarding sexuality, and he underscores the influence this still has in molding repressions, denial, inhibitions, and parents' inappropriate training practices with their children.

Conversion reactions are generally defined as emotional disorders involving shifting disabilities in various sensory and voluntary motor-muscular systems of the body.[3] In these disorders, the original emotional conflict—most frequently a sexual conflict, but occasionally an aggressive one—appears to be dealt with unconsciously: it is repressed, and after repression it is converted into a bodily disturbance. Such disturbances occur in functions of bodily structures or organs supplied by the voluntary portion of the central nervous system. The voluntary muscles and the sensory organs are ordinarily involved.

Conversion reactions may involve disturbances in motor function, as in paralysis, loss of voice, or motor tics; alterations in sensory perception, as in sudden blindness or deafness; disturbances in awareness, as in conversion fainting or convulsion-like phenomena; and disturbances in the total body image, as in intense weakness, bizarre paralyses, or other symptoms. Conversion reactions may also produce disturbances in the functioning of the upper and lower ends of the gastrointestinal tract, as in certain types of vomiting or fecal soiling; disturbances in the voluntary components of respiration, as in hyperventilation or respiratory or barking tics; and some dysfunctions of the genitourinary organs, as in certain types of bed-wetting, bladder weakness, or urinary retention.

In conversion reactions the symptom seems to be the symbolic expression of a conflict. It results in a partial solution, at the cost of illness and suffering but with unconscious secondary gain accruing to the afflicted person (as, for instance, from enhanced dependence). The anxiety aroused by the conflict appears to be bound to the bodily symptom, with little conscious concern being shown by the person. This lack of concern is widely termed *la belle indifference*.[4] The disturbances in bodily functions do not follow anatomical lines of voluntary nerve distribution (as they would in essentially physical disorders) but conform to the afflicted person's unconscious needs and his naive concepts of body functioning. In both adolescents and adults, conversion reactions most often occur in persons having hysterical personalities, commonly but by no means exclusively women. They also appear in persons of other personality types.

Conversion Reactions in Eastern Kentucky

Although some adolescents having conversion-reaction disorders were referred to our clinics in the four local health departments, a larger number from the area have been referred directly to the outpatient clinics and inpatient wards of the University of Kentucky Medical Center. I have seen a moderate number of these patients on child-psychiatry consultation in the University hospital setting over a six-year period.[5]

Our field data together with the University hospital data suggest that, in Eastern Kentucky, conversion reactions in adolescents constitute a mental health problem of moderate frequency. On the basis of crude data from the adult outpatient clinics and wards of the University hospital and from discussions I have had with family physicians in a number of Eastern Kentucky counties, I conclude that the same assessment applies to adults. The combined data indicate that conversion reactions occur predominantly, but not exclusively, in adolescent girls and young women. Occasionally, a teen-age boy or young man develops such a disorder. Referrals came predominantly from families in the lower socioeconomic class, or from working-class families.

The conversion reactions we most frequently encountered in both the field and hospital settings were "seizures," or seizure-like phenomena. Faced with seizures in one of their patients, Eastern Kentucky family physicians often wanted assistance in completing a diagnostic review. They then often referred such patients to the Department of Neurology at the University of Kentucky Medical Center. There, after the case was reviewed, close clinical histories, formal neurological examinations, and electroencephalographic data indicated the seizures did not have an organic basis. In addition, the doctors observed emotional conflict in these patients. Nonetheless, other family members were often convinced that these seizures were evidence of true epilepsy in their wife or daughter. "She's got the epilepse!" was a phrase we frequently heard.

Although this pattern was the most common, we encountered conversion reactions involving a wide variety of partial or complete muscle paralyses, urinary disturbances, and various kinds of disturbances of sensation. Often the family dynamics giving rise to the reactions were as dramatic as the symptoms themselves, as is illustrated by the following life stories.

Margaret, who was fourteen, was a coquettish girl with long

black hair and snapping brown eyes. She came from a working-class family who tilled a small hillside farm. The father augmented the family income from their annual tobacco crop by driving a school bus. Margaret, the oldest of five children, could do no wrong in her father's eyes—even when she took over all household tasks from her mother, a silent, self-effacing, inhibited woman. When her mother set the table, Margaret reset it. When her mother hoed the garden, Margaret rehoed it. The mother accepted Margaret's tyranny in abject silence. Neighbors put it bluntly: "She lets that kid walk all over her!"

The paternal grandparents had for years disapproved of their son's marriage, and they sided openly with Margaret both in her actual displacement of her mother and in her repeated criticisms. The father either gave silent approval to their humiliation of his wife or joined Margaret in criticizing the inhibited woman.

On entering the local consolidated high school, Margaret, a hard-driving, perfectionistic girl who had previously done well, was quite tense over the more difficult academic courses. Characteristically, she attempted to cope with her situational anxiety by attempting to discredit her homeroom teacher. At times Margaret tried to take over the class from this woman, in the manner she had employed all along at home. One day when her class was being given a test, Margaret directed a barrage of criticism at her teacher that sent the woman fleeing in tears from the classroom. Then, on the spot, Margaret lost her voice. She had developed an aphonia, a type of conversion reaction involving the voluntary motor muscles of speech.

The family physician referred Margaret to our local clinic, where she communicated with me by writing. Her symptom meant, she wrote, that she was contracting some serious lung disease, probably tuberculosis, as her paternal uncle had some years before. She anticipated leaving school and remaining at home as an invalid, cared for by her solicitous father.

Margaret suddenly regained her voice two weeks later. I had abruptly terminated an individual interview with the statement that I felt it was more important at that point to talk with her parents together. Margaret's first words were striking: "How dare you speak to them together! My mother isn't worth it!" Therapeutic progress then increased, as we helped the mother and father to unite more as a couple and as parents to put Margaret into a child-sized position. Margaret's anxiety abated, although for some time she continued to protest her parents' togetherness.

After completing high school as an honor graduate, Margaret married a teacher, today has a child of her own, plans on a career as a teacher, and has remained free from further emotional disorder. The emotional conflict in Margaret's life involved a continual acting out of disguised sexual, family-romance themes by all three key family members, along with an aggressive component. Open sexual conflict was frequently prominent in the lives of other children we saw who had other kinds of conversion reactions. Not all the afflicted children were girls. Some, like John, were preadolescent or adolescent boys.

John, age fifteen, was a passive, effeminate, rather fat boy from a poor family. John's father—quiet, passive, and peripheral —was frequently unemployed. At other times he earned a bit from odd jobs. John and he had never related well. John's mother was a chronic invalid with recurrent duodenal ulcers and menstrual problems. She moaned and groaned continually in a thoroughly hypochondriacal manner. Both parents acceded to the maternal grandmother's directing their affairs.

In early adolescence, John began to shun all learning and peer contacts. He gradually dropped out of school to remain at home assisting his mother with the cooking and household chores. After her announcement of her doctor's recommendation that she have a hysterectomy, John had to be sent to the University hospital with an acute conversion reaction—urinary retention. He could not void. Shortly after admission he developed another conversion reaction involving sudden and complete paralysis of his legs from the waist down. A day or two later his motor-muscular and urinary functions returned abruptly. Then, just as acutely, he developed false pregnancy. His lower abdomen was swollen for several days, and he groaned piteously with "labor pains." Clinical interview and psychological projective-test data obtained during this period underscored John's identity conflict, involving considerable psychosexual and sex-role confusion.

Judith, an early adolescent girl, presented still another kind of conversion reaction. Twelve years old, she was a timid, relatively quiet, mousy girl when one first met her. But she quickly thawed, forming quick, superficial relationships with men in a mildly coquettish manner. An only child, she was bright and did well in school. Her father, a swarthy, handsome man of thirty, had low-back pains and felt unable to work out in the community, where, in fact, no jobs were available. He remained at home on the family's small hillside farm, hoed the garden and tobacco, and ran his red-bone hounds up and down the ridge hunting rabbits and squirrels. Judith's mother, also thirty, worked nearby as a clerk in the county courthouse. Judith rode the bus every day to a consolidated elementary school.

Late one spring, shortly after Judith's twelfth birthday, her mother had an acute cerebral hemorrhage. Studies at a regional hospital led to the finding of an aneurysm at the base of her skull, which was successfully corrected by neurosurgery. At the end of the summer, after a fairly rapid recovery, Judith's mother returned to her work.

But as Judith began the sixth grade that fall, she was fretting over her mother. Separation anxiety mounted, and soon Judith was home with a full-blown acute school-phobic reaction.

Her solicitous father hovered over her. He prepared a daybed for her in their living room. There Judith lay, her right side to the wall. Her father often sat at her left side, near her head. When the girl complained of headache, he applied cold cloths to her forehead. When she anxiously developed a fast heart rate and smothering sensations, her father patted her chest, saying, "Tell me just where it hurts, honey!" And when Judith complained of butterflies in her stomach, he patted and palpated her abdomen.

At this point, Judith was referred to our clinic by the family physician. She had developed acute left-sided motor-muscular weakness and left-sided diminution of touch sensation. Both were conversion reactions. Formal neurological examination of Judith was normal.

Our speculation was that her father's repetitious examination of her left side was both sexually titillating and anxiety-arousing for Judith, who resolved the conflict by the unconscious binding of her anxiety in the reduced functioning of that part of her body most accessible to her father. That part of her just could not respond to him anymore.

Several adolescents referred to our clinics had emotional disorders consisting of either alternating or mixed psychophysiologic and conversion reactions. Their physical examinations, neurological examinations, and electroencephalographic data were normal. Review of the personality-emotional data on these adolescents indicated that current conflict situations involving either separation anxiety or anxiety over demands for autonomous functioning were present as precipitating stresses in the psychophysiologic episodes of these mixed disorders. At other times, the current conflict situations involved sexual wishes and fears and were the precipitating stresses in the development of the various brief conversion reactions. Linda was fairly typical of this group of adolescent children with such mixed disorders. She was eighteen—a tense, self-deprecating girl who wore an almost constant hangdog expression when she was around men in an unwitting effort (which was usually quite successful) to enlist sympathy from them. She and her mother, making up a middle-class family by county standards, lived alone. Her parents had been separated for the year prior to her referral because of the father's alcoholism and marital infidelity. Two older sisters were married. An episode of encephalitis when she was two had left Linda with a mild speech defect, difficulty in fine motor coordination, and mild muscular weakness of the right side of her face. Because of these slight neurological deficits, her parents indulged and over-protected her and sheltered her from the outside world. She grew into school age as a dependent, demanding, manipulative child. At times in school, when assertive behavior and autonomous functioning were demanded of her, Linda had fainting spells. At other times she persuaded others to do things for her that she could easily do for herself.

Since the parents had reinforced Linda's concept of herself as a handicapped person and had allowed her to remain immature, it was not surprising that as adolescence approached she withdrew increasingly from social contact with her peers. At this point the parents further hindered her development by using her as a pawn in their own conflicts. Her father was pleased at Linda's siding with him during frequent parental quarrels. He encouraged her affection for him to the point of being subtly seductive toward her. She, in turn, developed an excessively strong attachment to him. After her parents separated, Linda withdrew from school, and from her mother as well, and retired to her room to daydream about being close to her father. At rather infrequent intervals he came to the house to see her. During several of these visits she became anxiously elated and developed "seizures." These episodes began with numbness and tingling of her palms, followed by a period of semiconsciousness with tensing and jerking movements of her extremities. The seizures were terminated by the arching of her back, with several pelvic thrusting movements.

Neurologic examination revealed only the mild consequences of her earlier encephalitis; the electroencephalographic examination was normal. Clinical-interview and psychological projective-test data indicated that her unresolved conflicts revolved around a mixture of sexuality and hostile-dependent longings.

Nonverbality

In contrast with other clinic families, but like those with children having psychophysiologic disorders, the families of children having conversion reactions were relatively nonverbal. These families, including the children, had difficulty expressing intense or conflicted feelings. Many times all family members found it particularly hard to talk about the child's sexual maturation and functioning and about the current sexual conflicts in the family. As these older children and their parents sat relatively silently through early interviews designed to explore the problems they brought to us, there was ample nonverbal evidence that they were experiencing disturbing feelings. They flushed, frowned, twisted, blanched, or occasionally, if sexual matters were touched upon, developed open anxiety attacks.

Treatment Techniques

In family crisis situations that had produced conversion-reaction symptoms, our treatment goals were generally twofold. First and foremost, we endeavored to unite the parents emotionally, to assist them in regaining parental control over their children, and to reduce the sexualized acting-out or sexualized overcloseness between adults and child. This approach alone, if successfully worked through, often reduced anxiety in the family and the adolescent sufficiently to relieve the child of conversion symptoms. With symptom relief achieved, most of the families we followed dropped clinic contacts. Like other action-oriented families, they expected and welcomed help only in the symptomatic, crisis situation.

A few families remained longer in clinic treatment interviews. Now that he no longer had the symptoms, the adolescent was helped to understand sexual maturation and functioning more appropriately. At this stage we were active in aiding previously silent girls and boys to express their sexual wishes and fears. At the same time, the parents were helped to understand the necessity of eliminating or reducing sexually provocative situations within the family.

Causal Speculation

Two themes have emerged from our work with adolescents having conversion reactions. The first theme involves the parents' early training difficulties with respect to their children's sexual maturation and functioning. Though our survey of Eastern Kentucky child development suggests that this holds true for perhaps a majority of families in the region, in some it apparently is carried to a severe, potentially pathologic degree. All our adolescents with conversion reactions were struggling with anxiety-laden sexual conflicts, sometimes disguised, more frequently open.

The second theme, interwoven with the first, is that children with various conversion reactions, and their parents as well, were significantly nonverbal compared with children who either had no emotional problems, or had emotional problems of another sort.

Our clinical data suggest the hypothesis, I feel, that specific, unresolved sexual conflicts and blocked verbal expression of feelings operate together, or constitute the two necessary etiologic factors, in the development of conversion reactions in Eastern Kentucky children.

HYSTERICAL PERSONALITY DISORDERS

A majority of the adolescent girls—but only one of the boys— seen with conversion reactions in either our field clinics or the University of Kentucky Medical Center setting had underlying hysterical personalities.[6] After acute conversion symptoms disappeared, these characteristic life-styles remained. The hysterical personality as a common regional type has long been a subject of southern folklore, music, drama, and fiction. Margaret Mitchell's Scarlett O'Hara possessed such a life-style.[7] So, too, did Eve, the central figure of Thigpen's and Cleckley's clinical novel *The Three Faces of Eve*. Eve is of particular interest, in that at times of increased emotional stress she developed acute conversion or closely related acute dissociative reactions.[8]

The adolescents we followed whose life-styles could be

diagnosed as hysterical personality disorders had certain inter-personal relationship features in common. They showed ten-dencies toward flamboyant, overdramatic, overemotional, over-labile, coy, and seductive behavior. Despite their talk and frequent fantasies about overt heterosexual behavior, they gave evidence of unusual repression of sexual impulses. Within their peer groups the girls often exhibited superficial Carmen-like interpersonal behavior. Although they were superficially seduc-tive and they seemed socially poised, the girls usually experienced open anxiety in close interpersonal relationships with boys and men.

Mike, the one adolescent boy in this group, quite strikingly possessed a hysterical personality. A handsome boy of sixteen when I first met him, he carefully dramatized his muscular development and, in fact, his general appearance. He wore his black, curly hair in ringlets over his forehead, had long side-burns, and was growing a mustache. He liked sweaters, par-ticularly ones in vivid colors. I recall most an electric-blue one that had woven into it a white, V-shaped design from the point of the shoulders down to the navel area. Mike often wore his black karate belt over his regular one, to show me one of his interests. Actually, three prime interests emerged in his effusive telling of his life. He role-played his karate training and skills for me, talked dramatically at length of the swath he cut through the girls in his class, and became sweaty with anticipatory pleasure as he described standing at the pulpit on Sunday eve-nings in his Pentecostal church to lead his youth group in de-votionals. Mike also wrote poetry—well-written, highly sexualized poetry that, to cite one example, described vividly how ecstatic he would be when, at the height of his hoped-for career as an evangelist, he would stand erect before his audience and, at the climax of his sermon, experience waves of electrifying thrill speeding through his entire body. Others of his poems dealt with boy-girl relationships, rosy sunsets, undying devotion and passion, and flower gardens. Mike walked as he talked and wrote in a rolling, hip-swaggering gait that further dramatized his presence.

Actually, Mike's life-style was like his mother's. Although she wrote no poetry and performed no karate, Mike's mother had many of the dramatic, suggestible, seductive mannerisms of her son. She talked in a husky bedroom voice and seemed about to overflow the interstices of her black knit dress like a ripe plum. Her husband, Mike's father, was altogether different—a retiring, rather shy man who blended quietly into the background of the family's small farm. Mike and his mother had always been very close. She slept with him in her bed until he was fourteen, giggled and laughed over everything with him, and seemed to enjoy his seductiveness as much as he apparently enjoyed hers.

Mike was referred to our clinic by his family physician when he developed acute conversion reactions consisting of partial weakness in his legs, accompanied by numbness and tingling over the same area. The sudden onset of these motor and sensory symptoms occurred after church one Sunday evening. Mike had preached and led the group in singing "as I had never had done before!" Apparently this evidence of an "abundance of the Holy Spirit" in Mike moved his girl friend (their relationship previously had been on a Mike-talking-mostly, superficial level) to come up after the service, declare her fondness for him, and ask him to drive her home. On the way she asked Mike to park and neck with her. At this point Mike developed his conversion symptoms. The girl was naturally frightened and, since Mike could not drive in his state of partial paralysis, she lost no time in returning him to his mother.

Mike's symptoms obviously had occurred at a point of overwhelming anxiety. He was made anxious when the relationship with his girl friend moved from the superficial plane he talked and wrote about to a threateningly closer interpersonal level. In this way Mike, and the adolescent girls in this group who also had hysterical personalities, gave evidence that they were experiencing considerable difficulty in establishing their own sexual identities and relationships.

Judith and Margaret, whose conversion reaction disorders were described earlier, had underlying hysterical personalities. Linda, also mentioned, had many traits characteristic of this life-style. She also had many infantile-dependent traits: she was demanding, dependent, and clinging as well as coy, suggestible, and seductive.

As we followed the adolescents, we saw that it was fairly common for those who had hysterical personalities to develop new symptoms, usually varying conversion reactions, when under increased emotional stress. Beth, another girl who was alternately timid and coquettish, had waxing and waning conversion reactions at different times in her life. She despised her tired, careworn mother and idolized her father. A marginal farmer, he had been very close with Beth from her infancy, indulging and "petting on" her. In later years their relationship took on seductive overtones. As an early adolescent, Beth enjoyed her father's winks at her, his frequent tickling, and the occasional opportunity to share her parents' bed.

At the time of her initial referral to the University hospital, Beth, who was then sixteen, had an acute conversion reaction consisting of seizurelike phenomena. The "seizures" had developed suddenly in the local high school setting, just after an older boy, with whom she had been flirting, kissed her. The symptoms cleared rapidly. But Beth's hysterical life-style remained. A year later she took a part-time job after school hours as a waitress in a local resturant. In that setting she suddenly developed several conversion reactions, seizures accompanied by muscular weakness in her lower extremities which for several days made it impossible for her to stand. She gave the story of waiting on two college students at the table the particular day symptoms developed. One, whom she said she liked immediately, responded, inviting her out on a date after the restaurant closed. She accepted. While walking with the young man to his car, Beth had her seizures and crumpled with muscular paralysis.

In Beth's life—as in Judith's, Margaret's, Linda's, and those of the others—the current conflicts that precipitated conversion reactions were generally sexual ones. It is also true that lifelong developmental conflicts leading to the formation of hysterical personalities in these adolescents were sexual ones. Inappropriate training in sexual maturation and functioning characterized all the families from which these adolescents came.

PSYCHOSEXUAL IDENTITY PROBLEMS IN ADOLESCENT BOYS

Anxious Personality Disorders

Several adolescent boys who developed various conversion reactions, acute anxiety attacks, and generalized fearfulness had underlying anxious-dependent personalities.[9] John, the boy mentioned earlier with urinary retention, paralysis, and pseudopregnancy, was a chronically anxious person. These boys were chronically tense and apprehensive over new situations, such as learning in school or attempting to meet and relate with people. Many of them were inhibited throughout a wide range of personal activities. This inhibition seemed related to their extraordinarily vivid fantasies about anticipated personal injury. They had been generally taught from infancy to perceive the environment as threatening, as potentially harmful, particularly for men. Some had grown up in families in which men had been crippled in coal-mining accidents or had chronic respiratory or other ill-nesses related to their earlier work. More crucial for the boys' personality development than the injuries themselves were the attitudes surrounding whatever events had befallen the older men in the family.

The fathers of these boys were generally apathetic, resigned, passive, altogether presenting themselves as weak models for psychosexual identification for their growing sons. The mothers of these boys reinforced the view that growing into manhood is potentially hazardous, demeaning, or merely a prelude to failure. Many women either demeaned the role of their husbands or bemoaned the fate that had incapacitated them, or both. It was clear that these boys were growing up with major difficulties in establishing a view of themselves as growing boys and in manifesting age-appropriate sex-role behavior in the family, school, and community. John, for example, was as passive and currently homebound as his father. In addition, he had also clearly identified with his mother. He assumed a woman's role in limiting his activities solely to housekeeping chores, in taking on his mother's menstrual problems symbolically in his conversion disorders, and in his effeminacy.

Some boys with anxious-dependent, somewhat effeminate per-sonalities had been raised from infancy by women alone; their fathers had died, deserted their families, or divorced their wives. Men were virtually absent from the developmental picture. These boys often had several older women as training models—widowed maternal grandmothers, their own mothers, and some-times older sisters. In addition to anxious and dependent char-acter traits, the effeminacy of these boys marked the extent of their psychosexual confusion, and their difficulties in establishing appropriate sex-role behavior underscored the problem. Several of them had settled into a passive sexual role with other older boys and young men as one expression of their identity problem. A few were actively experimenting still with various forms of passive, receptive sexuality. Some had not yet had any overt sexual difficulties, but related with others like petulant little old ladies. The passivity of many of them had invaded the learn-ing process as well: they remained passive nonlearners at school.

Oppositional Personality Disorders

A large number of generally older adolescent boys came to our field clinics with a variety of symptoms, usually chronic learning and behavior problems, related to underlying difficulties in establishing a comfortable identity as a developing man. This larger group of boys did not develop conversion reactions, anxiety attacks, or other neurotic symptoms. Instead, they acted out their feelings of inadequacy as boys, or their low self-regard, in some form of chronic misbehavior. In general, the training influences in the lives of these acting-out adolescents were similar to those described for the boys with anxious-dependent personalities. In the acting-out group, however, there was an additional specific training model for the acting-out itself. Parents themselves misbehaved in similar ways, for example, or expected such behavior.

The older adolescent boys in this group[10] covered the anxieties related to felt inadequacies as boys by patterns of chronic aggressiveness. Usually they expressed their aggressiveness by oppositional patterns of a passive character—stubbornness, dawdling, plain negativism—although sometimes they were actively aggressive: driving dangerously fast on county roads, fighting with other young men, and aggressive spree drinking coupled with stories of personal aggressive prowess. At other times they appeared to be conforming, but they continually provoked adults or younger children in their own families. By the use of procrastination and other negative measures, they covertly showed their underlying aggressivity. When these oppositional tendencies invaded the learning process, difficulties arose from their failing to hear, to follow through and complete tasks, or to relate with the external authority of the teacher and principal. Many gradually dropped out of late grade or early high school, loafed around town, or in time migrated away from the local counties. Some were aggressive enough to get into difficulty with local laws. Many of them were then committed to the Department of Child Welfare and sent to the several residential treatment institutions or group work-camp facilities run by the department. There, through guidance counseling, training in real-work programs, and supervised peer relationships, many of these older boys markedly improved. Their identity problems, basic to their previous misbehavior and failure to learn, had been somewhat resolved.

Typical of this group of boys with oppositional personalities was fourteen-year-old Pete. A gangling, fair-haired, blue-eyed youth, he was a warm, almost personable boy in relation with others than his mother, siblings, and teachers. With them he was sullen, belligerent, defiant, and pouting. Pete's father, once employed in the coal mines, had been laid off when Pete was six. Lacking any other training, the father was from then on unemployed: he drifted between the rural county and Ohio, drank often and excessively, and when at home berated or physically assaulted his wife. Pete's mother, a careworn, chronically depressed, martyred person, had for years been unable to cope with her husband's difficulties. When he was drunk or gone, she constantly berated Pete, telling him that he would in all probability turn out like his father.

As a child Pete would cry when his father was gone or when his mother lashed out critically at either of them. As an adolescent, Pete stopped crying. Instead, he began to snarl back at his mother and, by displacement, at his teachers. His mother in turn took this behavior to indicate she had been right all along: Pete was indeed "no good at all." He lost interest in his studies and became increasingly absent from school.

Pete was jailed when in response to his mother's critical provocation he clouted her with a poker. From jail a commitment to the Department of Child Welfare led him eventually into a nine-month period of work-camp participation and group counseling.

After he returned home, Pete asked to talk with me again in the clinic. His self-regard was much higher than it had been previously. He thought of himself as a young man who could eventually learn a trade, marry and raise a family. Though his mother was unchanged, Pete spoke of his newfound ability to withstand her criticism of him, to "grow around her." He wished to return to school locally until his sixteenth birthday, when he planned to enroll in the regional Job Corps training program. Pete attributed his new feelings about himself to his group work-camp experience: "I learned there I was really worth something as a man!"

As was the case with several other oppositional adolescent boys we followed, Pete had made significant progress in settling some important identity questions for himself. His basic warmth as a person enabled him, in time, to relate well with men and other boys and to learn from them greater self-regard and better ways of handling himself as a growing young man.

CHAPTER 6

In the Clinic:
Communication
Patterns

The use of language in Eastern Kentucky presents some striking contrasts.
On the one hand, there are clear
indications that many people in the
region find verbal communication very
difficult. Theirs is an economy of
language amounting to sparseness.
The stereotype of the Southern Appalachian mountaineer as a silent,
taciturn individual is based on this
difficulty. Neighbors of these people
characterize them graphically as
"quiet-turned." In our field clinics,
we have followed a number of the
silent members of these relatively
silent families. The striking phenomenon is that the silent families exist
side by side with others who are quite
able to express feelings and ideas
sensitively in words. The silent stereotype simply does not hold true for all.

The other impression we have
gained is that difficulty in the use of
spoken language, where it exists,
crosses socioeconomic class lines.
Though perhaps more individuals and
families in the lower class and working class are notably taciturn, we have
encountered many persons with sim-

ilar difficulties in the middle-class group. Warren Thomas, for example, was one man I knew for several years who portrayed exquisitely, but painfully, these problems in using language as a tool. A civil engineer, he was thirty-six when we met. He had grown up in a small Eastern Kentucky railroad town and left home at eighteen to attend the University of Kentucky in Lexington. After graduation, he settled into a very successful practice in Lexington as an engineering consultant and bridge designer. He met and married a woman from St. Louis who, like himself, possessed superior intelligence. Warren's wife and their five children contrasted sharply with him in speech patterns. They were verbally aggressive, constantly talking, and richly abstract in their use of the spoken language.

Warren, on the other hand, was extremely taciturn. His relative silence seemed an integral part of his general life-style as an overly inhibited person.[1] He showed superficial passivity while relating with others, with extreme or pathological shyness, inhibition of motor movements as he sat, and generally marked constriction of his personality functions, including his markedly diminished speech. I had occasion to meet often with Warren. He had brought one of his sons, an anxious boy with some chronic behavior problems, for psychotherapy with me at the Child Psychiatry Clinic of the University of Kentucky Medical Center. When Warren and I talked alone, he was always extremely uncomfortable. Any pressure on my part for him to talk much made him acutely anxious. Yet he was a warm, personable man in spite of his personality constriction and relative silence. He seemed to wish for warm and meaningful relationships but to be inhibited from achieving them. His language problem reinforced this. His wife and children often criticized him for his silence.

Warren had grown up in a relatively poor but stable working-class family. Chronic financial pressures, chronic illness in several older immediate family members, and discord between his parents remained significant burdens for his family to bear. They bore them alone—in silence.

In addition to the silent individual, other indicators show that nonverbality constitutes a regional conflict in Eastern Kentucky. Although the data are crude, they are clearly significant. Our observations cover several separate though interrelated areas of language training and performance.

Many Eastern Kentucky families, particularly in the lower and working classes, set sparse speech models for their children. Such consistently presented training in silence is reinforced by consistent deficits in reading as well. Poor people, who are often illiterate or only marginally literate, not only cannot afford to buy magazines, newspapers, and books for themselves and their children but also have themselves been trained to place no real value on the written word. Accordingly, they have neither the means nor the inclination to read to their children, for example. Nor do they generally encourage the children to read to them, after formal schooling has begun. Where language is concerned, the training forces in many families amount almost to a vacuum.

The effects of this preschool verbal vacuum show up early. In the lower elementary grades, teachers are aware of the striking differences between the speaking children and the nonspeaking children, who are as well the readers and the nonreaders. In spite of some real efforts by many teachers in the region to overcome these deficits in earlier language training, little ground seems to have been gained; for example, the principal of one consolidated junior high school in Eastern Kentucky (grades seven and eight) told me recently that achievement test scores indicated that about half of her student body of 650 children were reading at a fourth- or fifth-grade level. These students, tested at the end of the seventh grade, were thus three or four years below national average reading levels. This same principal, too, confirmed that nonreading and nonspeaking were frequently found in the same children.

There is evidence that regional nonverbality affects many Eastern Kentucky adolescents and young adults as well. University of Kentucky and other Commonwealth university or senior high school reviewers in the state have long noted the depressed verbal test scores compared with other aptitude test scores made by many college applicants from Eastern Kentucky taking nationally standardized college admissions tests. Faculty members at various colleges and universities in Kentucky become painfully aware of the verbal problems of many of these low-scoring Kentucky students as they begin their course work. No less are these students themselves aware of their language difficulties. The courses the students undertake depend a great deal, of course, on the facile use of language. There is much to read, to organize, and to speak about with one's teachers. Most of these students with language problems pull through, but some fail because of these deficiencies. To attempt to counteract this nonverbal trend, and to hold the nonverbal student in school, several Kentucky colleges and universities have recently engaged remedial-reading and language therapists.

Intertestingly, students who have language problems that impede their progress in the academic curriculum often come into their own in the more personalized aspects of their training. They frequently possess interpersonal skills to an exquisitely sensitive degree. Their early regional training in family closeness and relatedness seems to pertain here. An outgrowth of this early training is their skill in observing and correctly interpreting the often-subtle nonverbal behavior of people who are relatively silent. Many of these students, in spite of marginal academic work resulting from their language problems, are able to find successful business and professional careers in fields requiring skill in personalizing services.

REGIONAL NONVERBALITY: CLINICAL EVIDENCE

We have found the blocking of verbal communication to be of paramount importance in the development of certain emotional disorders. This nonverbality is a consistent theme in troubled children having what I call the consolidated-school syndrome, in children having elective mutism, and in children (and adults) having psychophysiologic or conversion reactions.

The Consolidated-School Syndrome
During the fall and winter of 1964, the principal of Big Creek school, a new consolidated elementary school in Clay County, called on the staff of the Manchester Project for emergency consultations. The newly opened school enrolled 325 children who previously attended scattered one-, two-, and three-room schools in the surrounding hollows and coves.

Eight children were involved. They presented a markedly uniform picture. Since the beginning of the school term, they had not spoken from the time they left home by bus until they returned. In the classroom they remained frozen in their seats, would not say a word, and refused to move to go to the bathroom, lunchroom, or playground. A few sobbed quietly as they sat. Several furtively nibbled at lunches brought from home, ceasing when noticed. None attempted to read or write. Gentle attempts by teachers or classmates to intervene were silently ignored or actively shrugged away. According to previous school reports, all had apparently functioned satisfactorily in their former schools.

Home visits by the public health nurses revealed that most of the eight children, unlike their neighboring peers, had either never or only rarely been beyond the families' homesteads and the nearby schools. Furthermore, these eight families were considered extreme social isolates by their neighbors. Apparently the symptoms represented the children's attempt through silent withdrawal to cope with the overwhelming anxiety engendered by the abrupt, unfamiliar situation. This withdrawal persisted for two or three months, then gradually diminished.

Fred Eggan, a cultural anthropologist at the University of Chicago, told me that his study group had found the same symptoms under similar personal-social circumstances among extremely isolated Norwegian fjord children who were beginning boarding school.[2] In my discussions with Eastern Kentucky family physicans, I have learned that they, too, have encountered this same acute problem over the years. One of them seemed to feel that my term "consolidated-school syndrome" filled a need. "As far as I'm concerned," he said, "that term is now part of the regional language." Public health nurses, school administrators, and various public-agency heads from the industrial north-central cities to which Southern Appalachian people tend to migrate have observed the same symptoms in some migrant children.[3] In these instances, the shock of recent transplantation seemed to furnish the precipitating emotional stress for silent withdrawal just as it did for the Big Creek children.

Elective Mutism
Several children who had not spoken in the classroom for years were referred to our field clinics by their teachers. These children were not deaf, mentally retarded, or psychotic (we took particular care to rule out these problems, since mutism is frequently associated with one or another of them). In fact, they were intellectually bright and, other than having the habit of not talking with anyone except certain family members or perhaps close childhood friends, reasonably well related. Most of them were in the middle grades of elementary school; over the years their not talking with anyone at school had become

accepted by teachers and classmates alike as part of their particular life-style. Teachers promoted them on the basis of their generally satisfactory written performances in all academic areas. Peers included them regularly as silent partners in playground games.

Psychiatric literature originally called this nonspeaking *aphasia voluntaria* or *voluntary mutism*. M. Tramer described the disorder, which he termed *elective mutism*, as occurring in those children who speak only to certain people and not to others.[4] Two child psychiatrists, Einar Pustrom and Rex Speers, have reviewed three children with elective mutism who were diagnosed and treated at the Child Psychiatry Unit of the University of North Carolina School of Medicine in Chapel Hill.[5] These clinicians illustrate in their cases how knowledge of the family dynamics can help in understanding the development of elective mutism in a child. First, Pustrom and Speers found that elective mutism was only one of several symptoms of the emotional disorders from which these children suffered. Second, they found that the mothers of all three children had conflicts about talking. Specifically, the mothers continually trained their children not to talk about certain "family secrets" with others. The children, close-tied with their parents, adapted to the training model by not speaking with strangers. The electively mute children we saw in Eastern Kentucky were similar in family dynamics to those in North Carolina reported by Pustrom and Speers. Two of these children were Patricia and Barbara Jo. Patricia, a pale, thin wisp of an eleven-year-old girl, was from a working-class family. Her father was employed as a groundskeeper at a local Catholic boarding school. Patricia, the seventh of the family's eleven children, had refused to talk with anyone outside the family since she was four. In addition, she never spoke with her father, although she talked frequently with her mother and siblings. When visitors came, Patricia became extremely shy and ran from them. There was some evidence that her mother had been extremely close, indulgent, and overprotective until Patricia was four, frequently anticipating demands or statements and speaking for the child. Then the next youngest sibling was born and began to claim some of the mother's time and attention.

One family factor was most striking: Patricia's father was frequently drunk, and when sober he worked only at his job outside without helping his wife in the care of their home or their children. The mother was silently embittered by her husband's lack of support. More significantly, it seemed, she was profoundly ashamed of his drinking. The Catholic school people reinforced the mother's shame by their frequent criticism of the father's behavior and attitudes.

Because of her deep and abiding sense of shame, the mother began to caution all the children to keep their father's problems a family secret. They were not, she urged, to speak of them outside the home. The older children seemed to pay little attention to their mother's injunctions. Patricia, however, apparently heeded them well. From age four on, she ran from and did not speak with strangers.

A general training pattern seemed clear to us in Patricia's case. First, there was the mother's extreme closeness with her daughter, typical of Eastern Kentucky families. In addition, however, Patricia's mother provided two specific training patterns that, superimposed on the dependent relationship, were crucial in the later development of the child's elective mutism: the mother spoke frequently for Patricia, and she urged the children not to divulge the shame-laden family secret of their father's drunkenness to strangers.

Barbara Jo was another child who demonstrated these same dynamics. A freckled, friendly youngster of seven, she was attending first grade. The father, a construction worker in a larger Eastern Kentucky town eighty miles distant, could visit his wife and children only on weekends. Two older sisters were married and living in the Middle West. A sister, eighteen, and a brother, thirteen, lived at home with Barbara Jo and their mother.

In the summer of 1965, coincident with her enrollment in the local Head Start program, Barbara Jo became electively mute. This muteness continued into the first grade, when she was referred to us by her teacher. She never spoke with strangers, but continued to talk only with immediate family members.

In the clinic, Barbara Jo's mother related quite dependently with her child. She told us how close she had always felt and been with the child. In the later years of her marriage, as her husband had gone off to work and the older children had left home, the mother felt drawn more and more into the close care of Barbara Jo, the "baby of the family."

Beyond these developmental details, Barbara Jo's mother was initially quite reluctant to talk about the total family situation.

Considerable support was needed, with direct questioning, to uncover significant emotional themes. Gradually, some emerged.

A month prior to Barbara Jo's entrance into Head Start, her mother had taken a part-time job as a waitress in a local restaurant. She regularly took Barbara Jo with her to work. One particular day a somewhat rowdy group of young men came into the restaurant for coffee. One of them spoke with Barbara Jo teasingly, which the child seemed to enjoy. As the mother told us later, it seemed to her that "these men looked like the kind who drove around all day looking for girls." She told us she had immediately intervened, taken Barbara Jo from the young men back into the kitchen, soundly spanked her, and told her never, never to speak to strangers again. Her mother's intense concerns were apparently readily perceived by Barbara Jo, who heeded the anxious injunctions from that point on.

The training patterns responsible for Barbara Jo's elective mutism were twofold. First, there existed the general pattern of close, interdependent ties between mother and child. Second, a more specific pattern involved the mother's own long-standing conflicts over sexuality. She had grown up fearing sexuality. Her fears were particularly focused on strangers. Her frightened intervention between Barbara Jo and the young men in the restaurant translated her concerns over sexuality into the simple causal terms of "do not talk to strangers" for her child.

Each of the electively mute Eastern Kentucky children we saw demonstrated this twofold training pattern. Initially there is the trend toward closeness between the mother and child typical for families in the region. Superimposed on this, however, is a specific family reason of one kind or another for the child's not talking with strangers.

Although the total number of children with elective mutism reviewed by Pustrom and Speers and ourselves is small, our separate reports from North Carolina and Eastern Kentucky may indicate that there have been and are now more cases of elective mutism in children throughout the Southern Appalachian region than reported heretofore. If this is true, elective mutism in children would have a higher prevalence in the Southern Appalachian region than anywhere else in the nation. Although published reports of children with this symptom have come from around the country, the numbers involved have been smaller than the probable Southern Appalachian prevalence figures. Thus, elective mutism may actually represent another regionally significant emotional problem for Southern Appalachian children. Certainly, the characteristic family dynamics we have found in our cases have a heightened degree of replication throughout the region. Family-closeness training patterns, coupled with specific conflicts over shame and sexuality, are indeed prominent in many Southern Appalachian families. I suspect there are many more electively mute children, current cases and future ones, yet to be found within the region.

Psychophysiologic and Conversion Reactions
These two general types of emotional disorder, as we found them occurring in Eastern Kentucky children, have already been discussed. But I want to emphasize here how characteristic we found nonverbality to be of children with one of these disorders. Taken together, psychophysiologic and conversion reactions are considered by many to represent "body-language disorders." They—and we, from our own work—feel that the use of this type of body language is fostered by circumstances that make direct verbal expression of conflicted feelings difficult or impossible. I have previously speculated that blocked verbal expression of conflicted feelings and specific infantile-dependent or sexual conflicts operate together, or constitute the two necessary conditions for the development of a psychophysiologic or conversion reaction in an Eastern Kentucky child or adult. Thus psychophysiologic and conversion reactions furnish additional clinical evidence for the effects of regional nonverbality.

HYPOTHESES REGARDING REGIONAL NONVERBALITY

I have outlined thus far some of the effects of regional nonverbality apparent to us. School data and clinical problems illustrate the difficulties many Eastern Kentucky children and adults have in using words as tools. The sparseness of the language training provided by many families in the region seems clear enough. Evident, too, are the resulting deficiencies in language performance. One must wonder how language disorders of this regional magnitude come about.

I feel that at least four aspects of the functioning of the Eastern Kentucky family system deserve attention here. The first, raised initially by Thomas Ford, is that the family system is held together by norms of obligation and not necessarily by bonds of affection. Close, interdependent family ties involve training of the children in obligatory closeness; closeness frequently becomes a training end in itself. Situations that are viewed as potentially disruptive of close family ties are warded off. The existence of this trained-in feeling of obligation toward other family members, with an absence or at least an attenuation of ties based on affection, places a severe emotional strain upon individuals. This includes a sense of guilt: the person does not feel as he thinks he should toward other family members. This strain, Ford feels, may help to explain some of the intensive internal conflicts as well as some of the striking lack of verbal communication inside families.

Presumably, then, the most severely strained families would show the greatest lack of verbal communication. We, and others, feel that this explains why families in the lower and working classes in Eastern Kentucky, the families having the greatest strains from many sources, have the greatest problems in using words as tools. As one impoverished mother put it: "I can't speak, when all my burdens sit so heavy on my chest." This would also explain, I feel, why the most socially isolated families had children with emotional problems based on nonverbal themes. These children had fewer experiences of talking matters over with others than had their peers. Their social contacts had been largely limited to their own strained, silent families. Support for this view has come from the observations many have made regarding the spread of television into even lower-class homes. The children see and hear others speaking, even when family members cannot. Local teachers ascribe some improved verbal performance by lower-class children to the influence of television. It will be interesting to follow up on this increasing regional trend. Can we speculate, for example, that the incidence of emotional problems based on nonverbal themes will decline as language as a working tool is brought more and more into homes?

The second consideration about Eastern Kentucky family functioning that has implications for language training and language performance is closely related to the first. Perhaps it is simply a restatement of this first consideration. Child developmentalists have long been aware that a child's earliest training in speech functions occurs in an interpersonal context. Children begin talking, and continue to develop speech, by imitating the sounds and words of others. If those who train the child are relatively silent, the child has little to imitate except silence. Strained silence begets silence. In addition, strained-silent family members lack a most important tool for relationships with others, speech itself. With social contacts curtailed by speech deficiencies—frequently reinforced by educational and geographic isolation—older family members are often shy and socially withdrawn. Warren, the father mentioned earlier, was such a person—inhibited not only in speech performance but in the totality of his being. Viewed in this context, then, limited speech is often merely one aspect of limited total personality functioning.

The third consideration involves another dimension of Southern Appalachian lower-class and working-class family functioning—the individual's and the family's orientation to action as opposed to the verbal consolidation, organization, and planning of one's experiences: "Talk is cheap. Action speaks louder than words. A man is known by his deeds, not his words." This action orientation of the lower-class and working-class Southern Appalachian person is, Jack Weller and others feel, a logical outgrowth of the original mountaineer's rugged individualism and traditionalism.[6]

The fourth consideration is the considerable difference between the amount of language used by men and that used by women. Even in the Eastern Kentucky middle class we have found women much more talkative than men. In consultations with teachers, for example, the women generally speak before the men do, and they speak longer. "Talk is women's work" was frequently heard, and heard across socioeconomic class lines. In many families this differential has had educational reinforcement. On the whole, the girls remain in school longer than the boys do. Action-oriented boys and adolescents of the lower and working classes eventually become bored with the word-oriented atmosphere of local schools. Many of them drop out. Later, the better-educated women, with further training in verbal skills, marry men having far less formal schooling. We noted the frequency with which a middle-class Eastern Kentucky woman with a completed high-school or partial college education married a man who went no farther than the fifth or sixth grade. In such family settings, men defer to their wives' better verbal skills.

Even in their traditional recreational pursuits of hunting and fishing in the mountains, men are trained from boyhood to "keep still." The silence of men engaged in these activities is an asset. All these considerations overlap, certainly. But taken together, they have been a potent training force behind the language problems of many Eastern Kentucky children.

To emphasize regional training forces leading to language problems is to present only half the language picture. Non-verbal families in Eastern Kentucky exist side-by-side with other families who are verbal. Our clinical work in the Manchester Project clearly indicates that many individuals and families, including some of the very poor, are able to express feelings and ideas sensitively in words. These verbal people have been exceptionally able to use word-oriented casework, nursing intervention, and psychotherapy.

One poor family demonstrated poignantly for me how well many of them not only can talk over their problems and troubled feelings with others but also can sum up the ways they feel outsiders can best help them with their difficulties. Sarah, the young mother in this particular family, alternated between anxious agitation and tired, careworn depression. She had ample justification for both kinds of feelings. Just after graduating from high school in her local county, Sarah had met and married Tom, a young man whose assets included a fifteen-acre farm inherited from his grandmother, and a reasonable degree of intelligence, personal warmth, and charm. But he had three chronic handicaps. He had dropped out of school in the fourth grade, he had a congenital defect in both of his eyes that, by the time of his marriage, had progressed to the point of serious loss of vision, and, even as a young man, he was still tied strongly to his mother's emotional apron strings.

Shortly after Tom and Sarah were married, Tom became almost totally and irremediably blind. He could no longer work their small farm and the chores and gardening fell to Sarah. At this point Tom sought—and obtained—public-assistance support. Shortly thereafter, the couple had their first child, a sturdy, blond, sighted girl. After the child's birth Sarah became more and more preoccupied with caring for her, a preoccupation based on her anxious concerns that their daughter would inherit her husband's eye problem. In the face of what he viewed as his wife's withdrawal from him with his many needs, Tom spent more and more time with his solicitous mother. His absences from their home made Sarah feel even more alone, more burdened, and she began in frustrated rage to lash out at Tom. Vicious, destructive cycles consisting of verbal attacks on each other, followed by guilt-ridden attempts to reconcile themselves to their hard lives, were repeated for the next two years.

During this period the public health nurse saw that Tom and Sarah were in need of outside help. At that time local resources for marital counseling were sparse. The already over-burdened local public-assistance worker found that she could do little to help Sarah make better use of her allotment check. Furthermore, this worker had neither the time nor the training to assist the couple through counseling. But Tom and Sarah were approached in their home by their local minister, a zealous, reverent man whose skills, it turned out, lay more in preaching than in clinical pastoral counseling. Sarah, particularly, was made even more anxious by this man's well-meaning attempts to intervene.

At this point in their troubled lives, Tom and Sarah conceived another child; eight months later, he was born prematurely—and totally blind—at the University of Kentucky Medical Center. Understandably, what little remained of Sarah's world crashed at once. As her anxiety deepened, her new infant, affected by his mother's strained and erratic care, failed to thrive. He retained none of his feedings and established no regular patterns of digestion, elimination, and sleeping. He was a restless, colicky, vomiting, wakeful child with almost constant diarrhea. Repeated University of Kentucky hospitalizations were necessary. On the pediatric service the ward social worker attempted to intervene and counsel with Sarah, who seemed too frightened to relate well—which precluded effective casework in the hospital setting. The hospital pediatrician advised the local health department that daily visits by the public health nurse to the couple's home were necessary to interpret and reinforce the hospital's recommendations to Sarah, to demonstrate to this distraught woman the mixing of the special infant formulas needed, and to support her as much as possible in the hard task of caring generally for this difficult and disappointing baby.

Realizing her own limitations regarding counseling, and noting that the contacts with hospital personnel, the local public-assistance worker, and the local minister served only to increase, rather than to alleviate Sarah's anxiety, the nurse referred Sarah and Tom to one of our field mental health clinics. Mary Smith, a psychiatrist, began to meet regularly with the couple in their home. Dr. Smith soon found that she, too, seemed to be making Sarah more anxious by coming and talking with her. A crisis point was soon reached: Sarah in a screaming, frustrated rage barred the door against the local minister on one of his counseling calls. She went on to declare that she wanted no further help from anyone.

At this critical point—on the suggestion of Dr. Smith and the public health nurse, who had jointly coaxed agreement from Sarah—I chaired a meeting of all the helping professionals involved with the couple. Tom and Sarah came, too, with their two children. The professionals who attended that hour-long meeting were Dr. Smith, the nurse, the pediatric social worker, the local minister, the local public-assistance worker and her supervisor, and the couple's local family physician.

After we had discussed how distressed Tom and Sarah naturally were with their many problems, and how confusing and additionally distressing so much remedial advice from so many people must be, Sarah—followed shortly by Tom—poured out her troubles in a torrent of feelings and words. Then, following this sensitive recital of her distress, Sarah in brief words gave us all our professional marching orders. She knew what she needed and wanted. Furthermore, in the midst of their difficulties she had come to sense what role each of us could best play in helping her and Tom. It was a humbling but profoundly gratifying experience to hear her sort us out as helpers. She told the group she wanted her minister to stay in his church and to preach to her of God's love and support on those Sundays she felt "able to rise up and come down there." Sarah told him he could serve her best by doing this, and this only. She went on to say that she wanted the public health nurse to visit her "and hep me tend to this baby of our'n," but that daily visits in the past "riled me." The nurse and Sarah agreed on a twice-weekly visiting schedule. Sarah then told the hospital social worker to do no more casework with her, but "just come visit with me, Honey, when's me and the baby have to come down to Lexington." Finally, Sarah turned to Dr. Smith, saying that now she and Tom wouldn't "be so bothered" and could "get on, making do, with Dr. Mary." And so it went—as Sarah outlined it for herself and for us. Belated though it unquestionably was, our finally meeting with Sarah and Tom to *hear them* was the turning point. We now were responding to this couple's real needs, and we assisted them to cope much more adequately with their problems over the course of the next two years.

This ability to speak to their feelings sensitively is not limited to adults. Most of their children have also been trained to recognize feelings and to put those feelings into words. Ralph, a ten-year-old boy I met as one of our first clinic patients in 1964, convinced me, as others have since, that many Eastern Kentucky children, too, have these feeling-oriented verbal skills.

At the time I first met him, Ralph was a bright, appealing, freckled youngster who engaged me easily with a steady gaze and a slow, slanted grin. Underneath his friendly relatedness, however, Ralph was anxiously preoccupied with thoughts that rocks and trees would fall on him and injure him. He slept fitfully, was afraid of loud noises and was easily startled, had many nightmares, and was doing progressively worse in school. Although he had above-average intelligence, Ralph's anxious preoccupations took up the time and energy he could have put to his studies. All these problems, his mother felt, stemmed from the time Ralph watched helplessly while his beloved father, home on furlough from a state tuberculosis hospital, blew his own head off with a shotgun on the front porch of the family's cabin.

During that first clinic visit, Ralph and I talked a great deal about his problems and his feelings. In our second meeting he began to play with some of the toys I employed to further communication, particularly with younger children. Ralph seemed especially interested in a long-barreled, bazooka-type suction gun that shot out ping-pong balls. He fired it. The noise made him jump. Momentarily, he was pale with fright. Then he turned to me and said: "Doc, did you bring this-here gun just to let me play with it, or to see if I get feared of loud noises?" I recall commenting that he seemed to figure things out pretty well and could talk about them quite accurately. A week or so later, after much gun play attended by gradually diminishing startle responses on his part, Ralph added another insightful one-liner when he commented: "You know, Doc, I've got this thing figgered out. My Daddy skeered me pretty awful when he killed hisself with that-there shotgun, but Buddy, I'm not so skeered of this-here gun of your'n 'cause *my* finger's on the trigger!" In my previous years of psychotherapy with children I had not heard a more succinct, accurate, feeling-oriented expression in words of a child's seeing himself turning from a helpless, passive recipient of a frightening event into an active doer who can master and control himself and his environment.

Thus, when plans are properly made with them as active participants in that planning, many of these poor but feeling-oriented and verbal Eastern Kentucky families can make effective use of insight-directed, even long-term psychotherapy. For the nonverbal families that exist side-by-side with them, on the other hand, we adopted revised casework and nursing techniques. Crisis-oriented and brief-contact intervention, home-treatment services, and community-action projects were found more appropriate to the needs of these action-oriented families. Our clinical conclusion was that the treatment approach, including considerations for and against the place of verbal techniques in treatment plans, must be flexible and fitted to the values, attitudes, needs, and verbal or nonverbal style of the family we are trying to help.

CHAPTER 7   Family
Portrait

A gauntlet was thrown down before
us in the fall of 1964, early in the
course of our work in the field clinics.
At that time we were new in the
region—a comparatively untried mental health resource team for children.
Although our clinics in the local
health departments had been established at the invitation of the regional
health officer and her nursing staff,
others in local leadership positions
knew little about us. It was natural,
then, that the challenge was a family
that had baffled those who had tried
to work with it. The psychiatric
social worker for the clinic, one of
the senior nurses from the local health
department, and I had been invited
by the county school superintendent
to take part in a day-long training
program for local teachers. That
particular morning, the school superintendent and the three of us from
the health department shared the
stage in the auditorium of the county
high school. Each of us spoke of our
joint plans for the work with troubled
children. The reception accorded us
by the teachers, as I recall, was a
very natural one. Some were openly

enthusiastic, others polite but reserved, a few doubtful about us and the work. We made a strong plea that morning for the support of the group, underscoring our conviction that teachers know a great deal about children and should constitute a prime source for referral of maladjusting children to our clinics. That plea found its mark in a way we had not anticipated.

After the morning's program, we all met for lunch in the school cafeteria. There the teachers began talking about Danny and his family. Danny was first mentioned by several of his former elementary teachers. Then others joined in, eventually with feelings so intense we realized that this particular child and his family were the current focus of a well-known regional conflict, one encountered by most persons who have attempted to assist very poor families in any helping capacity in the Southern Appalachian region. It consists of the trained professional person's desire to help versus the families' apathetic failure to respond.

In the particular family being brought to our attention, the facts supplied ample reasons for the teachers' feelings of inadequacy, frustration, despair, and collective anger. Danny, then eleven, had up to that time been virtually unable to attend school. He seemed to the teachers to be painfully shy and verbally noncommunicative in the presence of anybody except an immediate family member. He had attended school a total of only forty-five days during the preceding five years. The pattern was always the same. Danny, pale, gaunt, thinly clad in filthy rags that smelled of urine, came only rarely to his assigned class. Sometimes he rode the bus to school. At other times he walked the mile and a half from his family's shack. The school building itself, a modern consolidated elementary unit, stood in stark contrast to his family's bleak surroundings. Danny would stay in school an hour or two, or perhaps a day or so, then silently drift off alone. He would play in the woods for a time, then return to his cabin. The three-room cabin, shared through the years by the thirteen members of Danny's family, stood unpainted, run-down, in the midst of refuse and weeds covering a slag pile. Five similar cabins and families shared this ridge, an area called Muddy Gap.

Danny's family, long known to school and health department officials, was economically and emotionally impoverished. So bleak was their existence that the crew of a Walter Cronkite TV program had chosen them in the winter of 1963-1964 to portray some aspects of Appalachian life to the nation. Many community leaders, including most of the teachers then telling us of Danny's plight and their own reactive feelings, recalled well the day the CBS crew worked in Muddy Gap. They angrily attacked the special program that had held forth Danny's family to the nation: "people ought to know that we are not all like that!"

How stark was this family's plight, how clear and understandable the teachers' feelings! We in the health department had been thrust into our first referral of a very poor family, and this referral carried a charge born out of the teachers' long-standing frustration: "Now see if you can do anything with them." Following this challenging request, the public health nurse who had been trying to work with the family for several years suggested that they come to our clinic. Their agreement to see us was an apathetic, resigned, compliant one. Although they understood that we wanted to learn more about Danny, in order to help everyone concerned, such an offer seemed beyond their emotional comprehension. Over a lifetime, stresses of all kinds had bowed them down. They seemed incapable at first of perceiving that there might be alternative ways of coping with stress. This was understandable—they had had few successful experiences of any kind. Virgil, Danny's father, was illiterate, unemployed, and chronically ill. Rachel, Danny's mother, was thin, gaunt, slumped, and depressed. The family was unspeakably poor, dirty, often cold, and frequently hungry.

They walked the three and a half miles from their cabin in Muddy Gap to the local health department for their first appointment. Danny was a frail, frightened wisp of a boy huddled between his parents and younger siblings in the waiting room. He made no sound as he followed me down the hall, and allowed himself to be led into one room while the rest of the family were taken to another for their interview with our social worker. Once inside the room, Danny collapsed on the floor, pulled his rags over his face and head, and sobbed quietly. When I attempted to touch him gently with my hand, or with a comment, he jerked in startled response and withdrew further. Never in that initial hour did Danny uncover his face or speak.

The clinic's social worker fared somewhat better in her initial interview with Danny's parents. Together, they had hesitantly sketched in the family's plight. Virgil, Danny's father, at fifty had entered into an overriding physical and emotional decline. Years of hard labor in coal mines as a digger and loader had left him a pulmonary cripple with anthrocosis, unable to continue the only work he had ever done. Himself a middle child of many born to extremely poor, unschooled parents, Virgil had gone to work in the mines with his father when he was fifteen. Now he had been unable to work for over six years. His illiterate background had prepared him for no skilled or more sedentary tasks. In addition, he was reluctant to leave the only home he had ever known—the slag pile in Muddy Gap. Other than small pay from odd jobs—few of these were available at that time in the community—he had no income for his family. Chronically depressed, Virgil wandered the few miles from Muddy Gap to the county seat to spend time on street corners, in a local poolroom, or on a bench near the courthouse. He seemed to retain underlying warmth as a person, but his apathy and the Southern Appalachian mountaineer's traditional sense of individualism, pride, and suspicion of outsiders prevented him from seeking welfare support or the medical care he needed. He had gathered his plight and his family about him in isolated suffering.

At thirty-eight Virgil's wife, Rachel, looked fifty. Her face was drained of hope. Her shoulders sagged under the combined weight of poverty and her family's normal needs. She seemed to move woodenly through an existence of personal helplessness and hopelessness. At times she worked briefly at housecleaning jobs in the community, eking out a bare subsistence for the family. But she seemed to have no physical or emotional reserves beyond this level. When an older boy dropped out of school to join his father on his wandering in town, she could say or do nothing. When Danny ran home from school, she slumped further in silent despair. Her younger preschool children ran wild, beyond control. She could not raise her hand or voice to guide them. Three of the couple's older children had been in foster care at a time when the family was completely destitute. Later, one of the older boys was committed to the Department of Child Welfare for stealing and was placed in a residential treatment institution. One of the older girls was mentally retarded and nearly blind.

Rachel's own personal background was similar to her husband's. Both were raised in poverty. Both left school in their early adolescent years to work, he in the mines, she at odd jobs. They drifted into marriage. Added to their youth, lack of education, and poor general preparation for marriage and parenthood was the increasing burden of a large number of children and Virgil's often inadequate income as a nonunion miner.

Our initial review of Danny's family brought several determinants of their life-style into painful focus. The local health department had for years struggled to provide good medical care for the family. Living conditions and the family's apathy forced such efforts into an often-inadequate, symptomatic, crisis-oriented pattern. Chronic illness in some form, reinforced by inadequate nutrition, affected almost everybody in the family. Their apathy, lack of commitment to any goals, and resignation, typical of the very poor in Eastern Kentucky, seemed partly a product of their impaired physical health and functioning.

On the other hand, the family's feelings powerfully reinforced these physical factors. The deleterious effects of chronic unemployment were keenly felt. Dread of illness with its cost was very real. Poverty, anxiety about today, lack of any hope for the future, a sense of defeat, the bleakness of their existence, and the failure of the children—all these affected Virgil and Rachel. Feeling himself a poor provider, Virgil had become frustrated, anxious. He withdrew into himself, away from his wife and children. While he wandered aimlessly, Rachel remained at home, depressed and withdrawn.

Danny's poverty, fright, and interpersonal withdrawal were painfully evident at our first meeting. Beyond these points, I could obviously draw no conclusions about his functioning as a person. I could only wonder how much the total strangeness of our setting, my strangeness as a person, and the difficulty Danny had in relating and talking with strangers combined to produce his frightened withdrawal. It was also obvious that I would have to see him further in a setting more familiar to him if both his problems and any strengths he might possess were to be properly assessed. I did not want to subject him to the terror of further health department interviews at that point. I would need to see him in his home in the immediate future.

The public health nurse following the family, the clinic's social worker, and I visited Muddy Gap on a sunny afternoon in mid-February 1965. The slag pile, the cabin, and the refuse of many years littered the basin floor of what otherwise was a remarkably scenic high cove. Semicircular, rimmed by pine-covered limestone terraces, the cove lay on the north side of a high ridge. From the cabin door we looked out over a river valley below.

The three-room cabin itself was intensely hot, dirty, and smelly. Two preschool children played with sticks near the sulfurous, red-hot coal stove in the center of the main room. The new infant, dirty, wearing gray diapers that smelled a week old, gurgled, rather happily, over a bottle of milk. The bed on which he lay was covered with rags and one filthy blanket. The preschoolers scrambled about, grinning, wildly impulsive. One of them got too near the hot stove. Rachel told him to move away. He shrieked, grabbed a stick and thrust it at his mother as if to strike her. Rachel's shoulders slumped. She said nothing to the child, nor did she flinch or move away from the anticipated blow. Bantam chickens moved freely into and out of the cabin. Several emaciated kittens, the mother cat, and a ragged dog called Snowball were being chased by the children. Grinning, six-year-old Wayne picked up a kitten and thrust it at me: "Want to see me kill a cat, Doctor?"

At our approach, sensitive Danny ran to the back room and hid under a bed. Wayne scrambled after him, then peeked out at me: "There's room under here for you, too, Doctor!" Encouraged somewhat by Wayne's unwitting role as intermediary between Danny and me, I began to pet the family cat and to talk wtih Wayne. The cat was perched atop a large pile of unused clothing that had been donated by missionary groups. I asked the cat's name. "She ain't got none—we kill her kits!" Wayne replied from under the bed. He said Danny was scared of me. I acknowledged that fact aloud, adding the comment that it was understandable, since Danny was "shy-turned" and I was a stranger. Bit by bit, Wayne and I talked Danny out from his hiding place. Gradually, still as much from his younger brother's encouragement as from mine, Danny went outside with us.

There Wayne and his younger brothers and sisters took delight in showing me their toys—tin cans, old spoons, boards— with which they had scratched out part of the hillside behind the cabin. Their wild delight in mastering at least this much of their environment was matched by elaborate fantasies of playing that they were miners, earth-movers, or hunters. Following their lead, Danny slowly, tentatively began to relate with me and to talk. He asked me to sit with him in his playhouse. A shy pride was revealed in a faint grin that creased his face as he showed me how he had built it from sticks, car fenders, old toilet seats, burlap bags, and scraps of tarpaper. He began to talk in affect-laden words as we sat there together. He spoke of the imaginary playmates who shared his playhouse. He played dolls with them, feeding them, he said, on red beans, water gravy, and oatmeal. His knowledge of the world about him was starkly realistic in many other ways. He described the mine drip from which his family obtained their water, his fright in school, how different many of the other children seemed, and his few moments of solitary enjoyment in the woods.

By this time, it was clear that Danny was not psychotic—a possibility I had considered on the basis of the one previous, distorted clinic interview. Equally apparent to me as a result of this home visit was Danny's deep sensitivity about the differences between himself and others, and his fright when he attempted to bridge the interpersonal and cultural gap. But in spite of his chronic shyness, chronic sense of personal isolation, and probable mental retardation, he had also revealed certain strengths about himself that day. He was reality oriented, could relate in time, and could be helped to talk about his experiences.

On our trip back to the health department the nurse was enthusiastic. She had seen small but significant changes in Rachel as a result of our visit. Rachel, she noted, had tried to wash her dress for our visit. She had torn a picture from a magazine and put it on one wall. Furthermore, she had smiled— even if wanly—in response to the nurse's supportive comments about the picture, the dress, and a clean bottle for the baby.

A certain sense of optimism about Danny and his family now pervaded our discussions concerning them at the health department. Before our home visit, our own feelings about the family's potential for change had ranged from mild doubt to strong nihilism. One staff member had put it this way: "Is this the type of family we can best help!" But the nurse's optimism following the home visit, reinforced positively by my own and the caseworker's observations of the family's strengths, gradually erased our own therapeutic apathy.

Together we had seen the family's problems. Their chronic apathy and lack of ambition seemed born of a depressed reaction to failures and frustrations. Their withdrawal represented a hopeless acceptance of deprivation that proved a psychological burden too heavy for them to lift alone. But we had seen strengths in the family as well: Rachel, Virgil, and the children basically liked and trusted their nurse. In beginning ways they had given evidence of capacities to relate with others as well as to trust them. We did not find, for example, the marked alienation and anomie which are frequent symptoms of this depressed reaction in the very poor as studied in several urban settings.[1]

We decided that the basic trustfulness of Danny's family would serve as our entering wedge, or prime factor, in helping them. It seemed to us that we had reached at this stage two conclusions of critical importance. First, our own therapeutic apathy and resistance had been brought into the open, faced, discussed, and worked through to the point that we now felt hopeful about the family. We needed some positive, optimistic attitudes in ourselves in order to communicate hope to them. Second, we had encountered the basic trustfulness of the family and could see this strength as a touchstone for our future work with them.

A third consideration now guided our planning, one that proceeded directly from the first and second. We decided that a reaching-out approach was indicated if we expected to involve the family in various activities and programs. There were indeed services in the county and state available for them: further medical review, temporary public-assistance financial support, a soon-to-be-enacted, oeo-sponsored Work Experience and Training Program ("Happy Pappies" program, in later local argot) for unemployed fathers, and schooling for the children. We recognized that if we were to help the family make use of these services, we would need to maintain a direct, personalized, warmly accepting, and encouraging approach with them.

Our plan for a reaching-out approach with the family was further guided by another important psychological consideration, one that involves ways of working with chronically depressed people. On the whole, those who are significantly depressed cannot easily talk of the intense burden of helplessness-hopelessness they feel or of the factors that feed their depression. To alleviate such a burden, someone else's shoulders must get under the feelings and circumstances and lift them. This means that someone else must first speak of the feelings crushing the depressed person. It also means that someone else must first show the practical way to cope with a particular situation that is reinforcing the cycle of depression. "Get under and lift up" is the axiom guiding such therapeutic intervention. Perhaps the words of one of our rural clients better describe this position: "If a turtle is pulled in, there's only one way to get him out. You put a fire under him." The two fires we decided to try with Danny's family were to talk about feelings and to give practical demonstrations of ways to cope with chronic stress.

A fourth consideration in our planning of treatment for the family involved the practical demonstrations already cited. Inasmuch as the attitudes and feelings of the parents were shaping the family's life-style and functioning, we decided that our initial intervention would center on Virgil and Rachel. Direct work with the children would come later. Accordingly, we discussed activities that might be meaningful for the parents. The concept guiding our deliberations here was the same as that of program planners who want to find ways of enlarging the horizons of disadvantaged children and youth, as in the national Head Start program. We wanted to explore with Virgil and Rachel activities that would have both an educational component and an immediate practical outcome for them. We felt that only in this way could positive, hopeful attitudes be promoted and more effective ways of coping demonstrated.

The final consideration in initial treatment plans was to choose the persons in the local area best qualified to meet with the family in the ways described above. Here we were guided by the phenomenon, long known to those who work with people in any helping capacity, that a troubled person frequently "picks his therapist." He may not choose the highly specialized and trained caseworker or psychotherapist. He may well choose someone else with whom he will share his feelings and from whom he will accept demonstrations of ways to cope with stress.

With this phenomenon in mind, we chose the public health nurse as the primary treatment person for the family. She had several unique advantages. First and foremost, she was not only familiar to the family but on the occasion of our home visit had been the supporting person to whom Rachel had responded. Only the nurse, comparing her home-visit observations of preceding months with the ones made at the time of our team visit, could see that Rachel was showing evidence of a beginning desire to improve her home and the care of her children. The clinic social worker and I were simply not familiar enough with the family to make appropriate comparisons and reality-oriented supportive comments based upon them. In addition, the senior public health nurse and the nursing students who worked with her were always present in the community. The family, if they were to be helped, needed someone almost daily with whom to talk, to act, and to plan.

At the time of this review of Danny's family, the county lacked other programs and personnel who might perform the treatment tasks we were then formulating for the nurse and her students.[2] Some of the staff questioned whether practical demonstrations with the family, which in the planning stage began to take on the shape of homemaker services, were an appropriate activity for the nurse. They talked at first of wanting to limit her intervention to traditional nursing programs. The nurse herself administered the final coup to this last stand of the team's therapeutic apathy: "The family has responded to us. They have not responded before. And I think you're right—they've picked me. There's no one else around here to help them. I'll do it!" The initial review and planning were over. Work with the family began.

The public health nurse—and later, under her supervision, successive Berea College senior nursing students on field placement—spent five or six hours each week with the family in their home. A direct, assertive approach guided the nurses' relationship with the family, particularly with Rachel, with whom the nurses worked primarily in the beginning phase of treatment. Structured learning and demonstrations involving the nurses' role-playing and setting up learning-by-doing projects were utilized. No abstract, insight-oriented methods were used. Each nurse talked as she set up these projects. She focused on underlying feelings that had made it difficult for Rachel to accomplish these things on her own. At first, the senior nurse focused on Rachel's own care of herself. She washed, shampooed, mended clothing, and demonstrated how makeup brought out some attractive features in Rachel's face. Apathetic at first, Rachel slowly began to smile as she felt less depleted. Initially she was a relatively passive watcher and listener as the nurse demonstrated personal cleanliness and self-care. Gradually, however, Rachel began to take over these tasks. She began to exhibit pride in simple accomplishments. Her slowly restored self-esteem led her to clean herself and her clothing. Once she had become somewhat self-restored, she could look outward to her children. She began to take pleasure in them and in her mothering role. With the nurse's praise and support, she was then able to clean them up as well.

After this much had been accomplished—it took several weeks —the nurse directed Rachel's attention to further tasks. She devised programs such as learning how to read recipes using the surplus-commodity foods distributed to many of the very poor. Another project consisted of sewing and mending the previously unused clothing given to the family by various missionary groups. A man with a mule was hired to plow up part of the lower hillside behind the family's cabin, and the nurse assisted in the planting of a small garden there that first spring. The children were shown how to help in the care of the garden. The nurse later demonstrated the canning of corn, tomatoes, and beans, and the drying of onions and potatoes.

Rachel gained real satisfaction from the appearance of better-cleaned, better-fed, now happier children. With the nurse's support, she enlarged her mothering role to include setting more consistent limits with her children. This afforded the nurse the opportunity to demonstrate effective ways of setting these limits. Gradually, the children responded by showing capacity to store tension, to delay gratification, to wait, and, finally, to respect the personal property rights of others. This had an effect on Danny. He responded with decreased shyness and isolation and eventually followed his mother's now-firm insistence that he remain in school.

At this point the nurse undertook an important additional task. Realizing that Danny's sensitive shyness and slow-learning problems would make his reintroduction to the classroom, and other outside contacts, difficult and slow, the nurse met frequently with school personnel to work out with them a program for the boy. Initially it permitted Danny to wander in the school almost at will. The nurse helped the teacher accept Danny's need for interpersonal distance at these times. He was allowed to choose first one classroom and then another. Within six months he found and accepted a special education class. There he gained some pleasure from his progress over several months' time to the level of a late first-grader.

Concurrently, Rachel wanted to know more about Danny's differences from her other children. She asked for, and got, renewed contacts at the health department for herself and Danny with the caseworker and me.

While the nurse and her students continued to work with the family in their home and with Danny's teachers, the caseworker and I saw Rachel and Danny several times each month at the health department. Danny no longer hid himself away. He continued to become less shy and began to tell me of happenings at school, climaxing these recitals one day by showing me, with considerable pride, the picture of his teacher. The caseworker and I felt that our contacts with the family served primarily to reinforce or support the nursing staff and the family in their work together.

Deficits in verbal communication within the family were gradually reduced through a number of other approaches. The nursing staff, the caseworker, and I gave careful attention to the way we listened to what the parents and children had to say. Being listened to and understood eventually brought them pleasure and made them feel that their efforts to communicate were worth the effort. Always, however, talking could be focused best around a particular activity. As the parents talked more with us, verbal communication with the children improved spontaneously. We pointed out to the parents the importance of family members' talking with one another. They could do this now, we told them, even though we might not be around to reinforce it. We felt that our praise of the family when they talked was perhaps less important in reinforcing verbal communication than our serious listening to them. As we listened, family strengths we had not previously seen became apparent. For example, we saw quick humor and quick compassion find expression in words. Their language was quite expressive, almost exquisite, in capturing events about them. As words were increasingly used, the family's relationships with one another and with us began to take on a less tense, more casual quality. More give-and-take was displayed.

For the first six months of our work with the family, the focus had been on Rachel and the children. Then, as his wife and children progressed, Virgil began to respond to the changes. He began to shave. He spent more time at home and less wandering the streets of the county seat. Later, at his wife's and the nurse's insistence and through arrangements made by the caseworker, Virgil went to the University of Kentucky Medical Center for review of his chronic pulmonary disease. Supported by the findings of this evaluation, he accepted a light-labor position on the Work Experience and Training Program (WETP). He was now earning $1.50 an hour from real work. He took more and more personal pride in his job, missing only one day in one six months' period. From his earnings he purchased for his

family their first refrigerator and first television set. At this point, the visiting nurse was often met by the delighted preschool children, who chattered about what they had seen and heard watching *Captain Kangaroo* and *Romper Room.*

Virgil's WETP sessions included evening literacy classes twice a week. With the nurse's encouragement, Virgil began to do related homework in front of the children. This had a remarkable effect on Danny, who asked his father to help him learn to read. Virgil and his son began to relate around such learning tasks. From the positives in their relationship came other effects. Virgil began to assist Rachel in household tasks, to help her with the children, to work in the garden, and to make minor repairs on the cabin.

These trends continued during the following four years. The effects of progress were both instructive and heartwarming. At present, the family's functioning presents quite a different picture from the one that confronted us five years ago.

Two years ago, Virgil moved his family to a larger, four-room house perhaps three hundred yards from the old cabin. He had considered moving away from Muddy Gap, but chose to remain in the cove that had been the family's home for two generations. He retains his regular job as a janitor in the local courthouse and continues to study in the evening. He cooperates with the nurse in periodic reviews of his own health and supports regular dental and medical care for Rachel and their children.

All the younger children, including Danny, attend school. Danny, still in his special education class, is working now at a third-grade level in most of his subjects. The family would like to send him to a local vocational training school in a year or two. However, vocational training in their county is limited to tenth-grade or older students who are doing well in their studies and to young adults. Even so, the family has considered an alternative plan for Danny. They may encourage him to enroll in the local Job Corps training program when he becomes sixteen. Danny himself is still somewhat hesitant and shy, but is a warm, personable youth.

Though the house they moved to is old and somewhat frail, Virgil and Rachel have done much to improve their living conditions. The house is dry and well heated. Brick asphalt siding and a tight roof cover the exterior. They have electricity. The house is adequately furnished with used, clean pieces.

Rachel keeps well-scrubbed linoleum on the floors, curtains at all the windows, and pictures on the walls. Each child has his own bed, with a bedspread, which is kept clean. Plastic flowers in glass jars brighten the windows. The children all have books and toys, and personal property rights are respected. Though the children still go barefoot much of the time in the dirt yard surrounding the house, they are made to wash up periodically and to keep their dirty feet off the furniture and beds in the meantime.

A new drilled well gives the family a steady supply of safe water, which still is carried to the house by hand. Rachel has a new washing machine and has learned to sew clothes for herself and the girls. Virgil has bought her a pressure cooker, with which she cans their garden produce. On one of my home visits in August 1968, she showed me with great pride the ninety-five quarts of wild blackberries the children picked for her to can. Virgil built a smokehouse and raises a hog each year for fresh and smoked meat. The bantam chickens and cats are no longer unduly teased by the children. Instead, the kittens are cherished and given names.

During my most recent home visit, Rachel made an observation that lingers with me. I feel that it speaks for itself, capturing the way she feels today about herself and about her family and their progress. On my arrival that day, the chorusing children had dragged their mother and me around to see the new pig. After I had seen their treasures they were satisfied and were off playing on a swing in the peach tree. Rachel asked me to come back with her to the house. After stirring the green beans she was fixing with pork for dinner, she directed me to sit down in the best chair in the living room. She sat smoking in the front doorway. Beyond her the sun was hot, but the air was unseasonably clear for August in the mountains. The fragrance of the pines was strong. The bantams clucked quietly near her feet.

We fell to talking quietly about the family's life over the past several years, and the problems that still face them. Our conversation reached one of those comfortable silences. Rachel, I saw, was looking from the doorway up at the rimrock edging the cove. She smoked. After a time she spoke very softly: "The hills are beautiful today. I'm glad I can see them."

CHAPTER 8   Some
Findings
and
Comparisons

At this point we need to turn to some
figures that give an explicit picture of
the kinds and scale of problems dealt
with by the Manchester Project.
Table 1 summarizes the data on the
psychopathology of the 287 emotionally troubled children diagnosed and
treated in our field clinics during the
initial six years of operation of the
project—August 1964 through July
1970.

The diagnostic terms used in this
summary call for some discussion.
First, the children referred to our
field clinics had been designated as
having emotional or learning problems by other persons in their cultural
setting. These were the public health
nurses, the local physicians, the children's teachers, or parents. Thus the
initial designation of these referred
children as maladjusting in some way,
by those in the region who knew
them, was essentially a culture-based
definition. Second, following our collaborative diagnostic evaluations of
these children the psychiatrists in the
project used for classification purposes

TABLE 1 Psychopathology in Eastern Kentucky Children
(*Children reviewed in the Manchester Project's field clinics 1964–1970*)

Type of Disorder	Number	Percent of Total Case Load	Male No. (Ages)	Female No. (Ages)
Reactive Disorders	80	27.9		
Anxiety reactions	25	8.8	10(10–18)	15(7–15)
Depressive reactions	8	2.8	3(15)	5(15–24)
Acute school phobia	33	11.6	16(7–16)	17(7–15)
Conduct disturbances	11	3.7	11(7–10)	—
Habit disturbances	3	.9	3(5–7)	—
Developmental Deviations				
Deviations in social development	14	4.6	5(2–4)	9(2–5)
Psychoneurotic Disorders	66	22.3		
Anxiety reactions	19	6.5	13(8–14)	6(8–11)
Chronic school phobia	20	6.9	11(7–16)	9(10–18)
Conversion reactions	17	6.1	1(15)	16(11–16)
Elective mutism	10	2.8	—	10(4–12)
Personality Disorders	95	33.1		
Anxious personality	19	6.5	14(9–16)	5(10–15)
Overly dependent personality	43	14.9	18(8–17)	25(7–19)
Overly independent personality	1	.4	1(10)	—
Hysterical personality	11	3.7	1(14)	10(14–18)
Oppositional personality	14	4.6	10(9–15)	4(14–16)
Tension-discharge disorder	3	.9	3(7–8)	—
Overly inhibited personality	5	1.8	2(13–16)	3(10–14)
Psychotic Disorders				
Symbiotic psychosis	3	.9	3(7–9)	—
Psychophysiologic Disorders	14	5.0		
Chronic diarrhea	1	.4	—	1(18)
Bronchial asthma	2	.9	2(12–15)	—
Syncope	3	.9	2(9)	1(18)
Eczema	1	.4	—	1(15)
Duodenal ulcer	3	.9	—	3(15–16)
Psychogenic vomiting	4	1.4	1(9)	3(7–15)
Brain Syndromes	4	1.4		
Minimal diffuse brain damage	3	.9	3(8–9)	—
Dyslexia	1	.4	1(13)	—
Mental Retardation	11	3.7	7(7–15)	4(9–17)
TOTALS	287		141	146

the new diagnostic nomenclature for psychopathological disorders of children recently recommended and outlined by the Committee on Child Psychiatry of the Group for the Advancement of Psychiatry.[1]

Socioeconomic data obtained from the families of these children placed them within the three-class social system characteristic of the Southern Appalachian region. The following information summarizes this socioeconomic data.

Total group of children: 287. *Age group:* 14 children were under 6; 154 were 6-12; 106 were 13-17; 9 were 18-24; 4 were over 24. *Sex:* 141 were boys; 146 were girls. *Race:* all children were Caucasian with the exception of one Negro child of 17. *Religion:* 152 families were Baptist; 10 were members of the Christian Church; 6 were Presbyterian; 42 were members of either the Holiness Church, Church of God, Nazarene Church, Pentecostal Church, or Jehovah's Witnesses; one family was Catholic; 37 had no church affiliation; in 39 religious affiliation was not known. *Marital status of parents:* 181 households included were married; 15 widowed; 32 divorced; 59 separated. *Household composition:* 151 were two-parent, nuclear families; 43 were one-parent, nuclear families; 30 were two-parent, extended families; 44 were one-parent, extended families; in 10 families the child was living with relatives (non-parent); in 10 cases the child was living in a foster home or boarding school. *Housing:* 163 families were in standard housing; 124 families were in housing considered substandard nationally (most lacked flush toilets and hot and cold running water; many lacked electricity and refrigeration). *Public-assistance status of head of household:* 183 had never applied; 23 were former recipients; 81 were active or pending recipients. *Household income level:* 79 families had incomes of less than $50.00 a week; 70 were at the public-assistance level; 117 had modest but adequate incomes; 21 were above the modest but adequate level. *Household income source:* 162 families had incomes from regular earnings; 25 from sporadic earnings; 71 were on public assistance; 21 were on pension or allotment; 8 were on social security, supported by relatives, or a combination of the above. *Education of head of household:* 15 had no schooling; 84 had completed grades 1-4; 80 had completed grades 5-6; 36 had completed grades 7-8; 34 had completed grades 9-11; 22 completed high school; 2 attended business or technical school; 7 attended college; 7 completed college. *Employment or occupation of head of household:* 17 owned their own businesses; 3 were ministers; 53 were small-farm owners; 14 were office clerks; 7 were teachers; 56 were coal miners; 18 were truck drivers; 23 were farm laborers; 24 were construction workers or in allied fields; 12 were engaged in some type of domestic service; 54 were chronically unemployed; 3 were retired; 3 subsisted from odd jobs.

TABLE 2 Psychopathology in Eastern Kentucky Children
(Children reviewed in case-consultations at the University of Kentucky Medical Center, 1964–1968)

Type of Disorder	Number	Percent of Total Case Load	Male No. (Ages)	Female No. (Ages)
Reactive Disorders	13	11.4		
Anxiety reactions	5	4.4	3(12–14)	2(11–14)
Acute school phobia	7	6.2	2(8–9)	5(7–12)
Depressive reactions	1	.8	1(10)	—
Developmental Deviations				
Deviations in social development	12	10.6	5(3–5)	7(3–5)
Psychoneurotic Disorders	22	19.2		
Conversion reactions	19	16.8	2(12–15)	17(10–17)
Anxiety reactions	1	.8	1(10)	—
Elective mutism	2	1.6	—	2(8–11)
Personality Disorders	28	24.6		
Anxious personality	6	5.3	2(12–14)	4(10–15)
Over dependent personality	12	10.6	7(7–16)	5(8–13)
Hysterical personality	3	2.6	1(16)	2(14–15)
Oppositional personality	6	5.3	5(8–13)	1(14)
Tension-discharge disorder	1	.8	1(14)	—
Psychotic Disorders	0			
Psychophysiologic Disorders	22	19.7		
Psychogenic vomiting	9	7.9	—	9(6–14)
Psychogenic headache	1	.8	—	1(13)
Eczema	1	.8	—	1(15)
Duodenal ulcer	1	.8	1(14)	—
Encopresis (fecal soiling)	5	4.4	3(6–9)	2(10–15)
Ulcerative colitis	2	1.6	—	2(11–12)
Bronchial asthma	2	1.6	1(5)	1(16)
Syncope	1	.8	—	1(10)
Brain Syndromes	10	8.5		
Minimal diffuse brain damage	6	5.3	4(7–8)	2(8–11)
Epilepsy	1	.8	—	1(15)
Toxic delirium	2	1.6	1(13)	1(9)
Dyslexia	1	.8	—	1(8)
Mental Retardation	6	5.3	3(3–16)	3(4–9)
TOTALS	113		43	70

In addition to the data summarized above, an additional
source of information about Eastern Kentucky families was
available to me over much of the same period of time. I refer
here to that relatively large number of children from the region
who presented complex medical problems for differential diag-
nosis to their local physicians. Many of these children needed
special review to complete a comprehensive diagnostic evaluation of their problems. Accordingly, they were often referred
to the University of Kentucky Medical Center's inpatient wards
or various specialty clinics by their local physicians. Between
July 1964 and July 1968, I had the opportunity to review many
of these children in the University hospital. This review was in
the form of child psychiatry case-consultations. The children
were selected for psychiatric consultation by their attending
physicians at the University hospital, who felt emotional factors
were prominent in the problems presented.

Table 2 summarizes the diagnostic data on this group of
children.

SOME CONCLUSIONS

The clinical psychopathological data on the Eastern Kentucky
children whom we reviewed, either in our field clinics or in
the University of Kentucky Medical Center, present some important points about the kinds of mental health problems children
have in this region. The conclusions are, of course, my own
and are subject therefore to some degree of interpretive error.
Nonetheless, some summary statements can be made:

1. Because of early case-finding and prompt referral by the
nursing staff, more Eastern Kentucky children with developmental problems or reactive disorders were seen in our field
clinics than would be seen ordinarily in many university or
urban-community child psychiatry clinics.

2. Eastern Kentucky family functioning in most instances was
markedly interdependent; their orientation was strongly familistic, often with extensive kinship ties. This factor, we felt,
related to the markedly increased incidence of dependency-
related psychopathology in Eastern Kentucky children, such as
acute and chronic school-phobic reactions, deviations in social
development, overly dependent personality disorders, symbiotic

psychosis, and various psychophysiologic reactions, as measured against data from a comparison group of mainly urban children reviewed in the Child Psychiatry Clinic at the University of Kentucky Medical Center.

3. There was a markedly increased incidence in children of psychopathology based in an essential way on conflicts over sexual maturation and functioning, such as conversion reactions, hysterical personality disorders in adolescent girls, and various other kinds of ·personality disorders in adolescent boys, as measured against data from the same urban comparison group.

4. There was an increased incidence of psychopathology in children from Eastern Kentucky related wholly or in part to conflicts over verbal communication, such as elective mutism, what I call the consolidated-school syndrome, and various psychophysiologic and conversion reactions, as measured against data from the same comparison group.

5. The remaining kinds of psychopathology in children from Eastern Kentucky, such as various chronic brain syndromes, primary mental retardation, and some forms of psychoneurotic disorders, were not strikingly different in form or incidence of occurrence from those in children seen at many urban child psychiatry clinics, including the Child Psychiatry Clinic at the University of Kentucky Medical Center.[2]

6. The combined psychopathological data presented here on this relatively large number of Eastern Kentucky children do not represent epidemiological or prevalence data for such mental disorders. In fact, no epidemiologic studies on mental disorders for either adults or children have ever been done in the Southern Appalachian region. However, our six-year data on psychopathology in children make up the longest and largest, with reference to the numbers of children followed longitudinally, currently available from the region.

The strikingly increased incidence of certain kinds of mental disorder in the Eastern Kentucky children we followed provided the basis for the selection of individual cases discussed in the preceding chapters.

THE VALUE, FUTURE, AND EFFECT OF THE
MANCHESTER PROJECT

Important as an understanding of the psychopathology or mental health problems of children in Eastern Kentucky may be, it is on the mobilization of local and other resources to attempt to prevent or to correct such problems that attention needs to be focused. Here again, the work of the local health officer and the senior public health nurses of the four-county region in which we worked bears reference.

Community Mobilization for Mental Health Services
First of all, the public health nurses accorded their work in our field mental health clinics the same importance they gave to other, perhaps more traditional, nursing programs. Furthermore, this interest of theirs, which initially sparked the development of local mental health diagnostic-treatment services for children in their area, has been sustained through our joint work of the past six years and is projected ahead. To our collective resources of knowledge and some expertise, the nurses have added compassion, the willingness to work in concert, agreement on the methods we used, and persistence.

Second, this interest of the nurses has had an effect on their communities through the years, with respect to local mental health planning. Several of the nurses have been active in the planning for regional mental health-mental retardation services for the entire population in their part of Eastern Kentucky. Some are members of regular advisory councils of these emerging regional service programs. Other nurses have actively promoted further local community action for service programs that have an important bearing on children's development and mental health. One organized a local chapter of a national body of parents of mentally retarded children. Another volunteered to be the nursing consultant for one county's OEO-sponsored Day Care program for children from very poor families. Still another nurse saw the need for additional special education classes for mentally retarded and neurologically handicapped children in her county. These classes were later funded and staffed.

Training Functions of the Manchester Project
Within the community clinic setting, through diagnostic evaluations and consultations, through various treatment methods, and in case, interagency, and family conferences, the residents in general psychiatry from the University of Kentucky were given supervised field experience in community child psychiatry. The residents learned to work collaboratively with children and their families, public health nurses, school personnel, public-assistance workers, and the local family physicians of the four-county region. The social work students and the senior nursing students

from Berea College were afforded similar collaborative field training and experience. A training seminar for personnel which I and the psychiatric social worker conducted concluded each field clinic. These seminars covered psychosocial development of children, family-process theory, theory and practice of school consultations, and psychodynamics and treatment as related to clinic cases. The focus was on sharpening and upgrading the knowledge and skills of project personnel.

In addition, the Manchester Project, like some other community mental health programs,[3] has served as a demonstration for various Commonwealth of Kentucky public-service agencies. Discussion of the operation of the project's field clinics continues in several other states as well. By focusing upon the intrinsic mental health component of public health work the project, we feel, has demonstrated one effective way of meeting at least partially the mental health needs of a community in a rural, impoverished area.

Two general themes are characteristic of the Manchester Project. The first is that in some respects the project resembles a traditionally organized community mental health clinic for children. It retains the elements of collaborative work in evaluations, community consultations, and treatment methods shared by all community clinics.

The second theme is that in other important respects the project makes a major departure from the more traditional community clinic model by taking its place with other public health programs in a county health department setting. Four elements of this setting are crucially important in the formation, continuing operation, and development of the project. First, the four health departments lead in comprehensive planning for all health services in the four-county region. Second, the health departments, their staffs, and their programs have strong professional and public acceptance. Third, the public health nurses represent what Hyman M. Forstenzer calls the most effective, community-oriented "technological agents" present in the region for modifying the amount of mental disorder in the population.[4] Fourth, the programs of the health departments have broad implications for primary, secondary, and tertiary prevention of mental disorders.

CHAPTER 9   Some
Development
Conclusions

When we launched the Manchester
Project in 1964, we spent a good deal
of time in reviewing the sociology of
Eastern Kentucky and in making a
field survey of child development in
the region. Both the review and the
survey were undertaken for purely
pragmatic reasons. As a clinical team,
we needed to understand how families
in the region raise normal children,
children able to cope relatively successfully with various developmental
tasks. Such an understanding would
give us a clinical yardstick for measur-
ing (not in a precise sense, of course)
the successes and failures in life adjustment of the children referred to
the field clinics.

As time passed, however, and more
and more clinical data accumulated,
we began to see some linkages between regional developmental themes
and both the psychopathology and
the ego strengths of the children.
Ultimately, then, our work in the
clinics and my approach in this writing rest, in their broader aspects, upon
the proposition that to understand
Eastern Kentucky's children, their

problems and their prospects, it is necessary to look at the entire field of regional developmental forces. Which ones are involved in change? Which ones tend to cause stagnation? But this cannot be done simply with a wide speculative view. It is necessary to look intensively into at least some of the more critical components of regional child development. On the basis of what I have done thus far, I feel able now to raise some correlations between development and its outcome—the derivatives of that development for children.

REGIONAL CULTURE AND MENTAL DISORDER

The frequency and severity of various psychopathological symptoms in any given population are probably affected very strongly by social relations and cultural values.[1] Those who have a strong social learning theory orientation to child development, as I do, tend to view mental disorder as primarily involving learned behaviors, which are reinforced by environmental influences.[2]

The structure of adult society and the function of the family unit within this larger framework provide a context within which the growing child interprets his experience. This context also provides a kind of mental set with which both the child and the adult approach new experiences. Viewed in this manner, regional training patterns, which vary from one region or one culture to another, are economical. The consistency with which they are set and maintained is important, of course. It allows us to be comfortable in our own environment. It facilitates the acquisition of generally efficient behaviors we describe as acculturation or socialization.

Although consistently presented regional training patterns make for learned, efficient behaviors in people within their cultural setting, the same training processes can also make it uncomfortable for the individual when change is called for.[3] Thus, an infantilized Eastern Kentucky child, for example, may adapt without much anxiety to an overprotective home environment during his preschool years; after starting school, he may become anxious when previously learned dependent behaviors run counter to the school's request that he function more assertively and more autonomously.

Those who have worked with Southern Appalachian migrants

in urban settings are aware of this same phenomenon, which may occur in one or more family members after the family changes cultural location. I learned a great deal about the kind of struggle that many migrants have from my work with Tracy Napier, a former coal miner from southeastern Kentucky.

During 1962 I had the opportunity to talk weekly with Tracy, a forty-two-year-old construction laborer, at the Central Psychiatric Clinic in Cincinnati. This man had moved his family from Harlan, in southeastern Kentucky, to a working-class suburb of Cincinnati one year previously. The family was referred for psychiatric care when the oldest son manifested an adolescent identity crisis and Tracy's wife simultaneously became psychotically depressed. The boy felt "strange and different" among his new high school classmates. He developed acute anxiety attacks and dissociative reactions in which he felt he was no longer himself. His mother, a silent, apathetic person, had been accepted as being "quiet-turned" by her Harlan neighbors. After the family's move to Ohio, her new working-class neighbors pressed her for interpersonal participation in a bowling league and their kaffeeklatsches. She could not easily adapt to the new role that the community expected her to play. Anxiety mounted, leading to despair and eventually to her depressive illness.

Tracy had been raised in a coal-mining family. His father was a verbally silent person who expressed himself by direct aggressive action. When Tracy was rebellious in early adolescence, for example, his father would knock him off the cabin porch with his fist or a two-by-four. Tracy identified strongly with, or patterned himself after, this action-oriented model. In his own marriage he cuffed his wife about and beat his children. Gradually, he became aware through his talks with his neighbors and fellow workers in Ohio that such role behavior was not altogether acceptable. This demand for change in behavior versus the inflexible training pattern of his youth created considerable conflict for this man. He developed anxiety attacks in my office as we talked about it.

Such a family as Tracy's may adjust in a marginally satisfactory way within the culture of origin for years, developing overt psychopathological symptoms only after a move to a cultural setting which demands new behaviors. Tracy's family is significant in that all three key members experienced adjustive difficulties in their new setting. One must wonder how many other Southern Appalachian migrant families experience similar problems—a question of first importance because of the great out-migration from the region during the past several decades.

In Eastern Kentucky, as in most regions, the major culture is predominantly the adult culture. What the children learn is strongly held to be useful to them later on as adults. The training patterns, or models for their children's behavior, provided by families in the region are relatively undiluted by social institutions outside the family. As Thomas Ford has pointed out, the extended family system is the only major, viable social unit in the Southern Appalachian region. It therefore holds a unique place as a children's training climate. And more often than not, the few social institutions available outside the family have, up to now, frequently served only to reinforce the family's training patterns.

Eastern Kentucky child-development training patterns appear to have been remarkably consistent within the region through several generations. We need now to take a second look at several of the most prominent training themes, considering each one again with reference to its implications for the mental health of children. These themes were presented in considerably more detail in the earlier chapters. I present them here in summary form to raise, speculatively, the connections that appear to exist between regional child development and regional psychopathology in children.

REGIONAL TRAINING IN DEPENDENCY

Long known to those who have worked in the Southern Appalachian region is the strong familistic orientation of the area's lower and middle classes, and to some extent of the area's upper class. Close, interdependent functioning is the major dynamic characteristic of these families. They are markedly inner-directed, with an overriding sense of obligation to extended-family members. Within such a family system, children are taught from birth in both verbal and nonverbal ways to maintain this close family system itself. They are taught to maintain it even at the expense of an individual family member's personal-social maturation. The individual's own growth and development is clearly subordinated to the prime task of maintaining the family as a close unit.

I speculate that the close, interdependent functioning of

Southern Appalachian families is trained into their children beginning with the developmental pattern of parental over-emphasis on the infancy period itself. This early pattern is strongly reinforced by the persistence of the families' infantile modes of relating with their children through subsequent stages of the children's development and by parental patterns of developmental underemphasis on children's autonomy, initiative, curiosity, exploration, and adequate sex-role differentiation.

Clearly related to this training theme of close, interdependent family functioning, we have felt from our clinical data, is the great frequency with which separation anxiety is a major emotional conflict faced by Eastern Kentucky children and by their parents. Actual, threatened, or symbolic disruptions in parent-child and other family relationships cause great concern. We found separation anxiety the most prominent causal conflict in children coming to us with the following psychopathological disorders: acute and chronic school-phobic reactions, overly dependent personality disorders, deviations in social development, symbiotic psychosis, various psychophysiologic reactions, and the consolidated-school syndrome. Further, our clinical data suggest a strikingly higher incidence for such dependency-related disorders in children from Eastern Kentucky than occurs in largely urban children referred to the Child Psychiatry Clinic at the University of Kentucky Medical Center in Lexington. The University of Kentucky clinic's cases are thus used as a crude comparison group for the children seen in our field clinics. The field data clearly show that this particular type of dependency-related psychopathology is a regional problem of great frequency.

As we examined the current interactional patterns and earlier training patterns of families having a child with one of these disorders, we found marked evidence of training in obligatory family closeness, coupled with rigorous training in avoiding separation that would disrupt the close family system. We felt that this training trend in the clinic families represented an exaggerated degree of, or pathogenic overuse of, that focus on infancy and regional training in closeness noted by us, in our survey of Eastern Kentucky child development, and by others.

Equally striking to us as we worked with children having various dependency-related disorders was the absence of certain disorders (early infantile autism, primary behavior disorders) based wholly or in large part on emotional deprivation in infancy.

These latter disorders simply did not appear in our clinic children.

What our data, therefore, seem to suggest, is the following hypothesis: regional familism (training in close, interdependent family functioning), when overused by families in training their children, is a strong, specific force in shaping those later psychopathological disorders in the children based on dependency themes and related separation anxiety. Furthermore, the same regional familism precludes the formation of those specific types of children's psychopathology based on extreme emotional deprivation in infancy.

REGIONAL TRAINING IN PSYCHOSEXUAL CONFLICT

A second prominent training theme or pattern in Eastern Kentucky emerges from the conflict concerning sexual development, maturation, and functioning. It was experienced by the great majority of the families we studied in our survey of normal child development. Although it was found in all socioeconomic classes, the conflict seemed most acute in lower-class and working-class families, for whom the open overcrowding necessitated by poverty created considerable sexual as well as other kinds of tensions. It is also true, as previous writers have emphasized, that the prevalent strict Protestant ethos is a powerful force in maintaining a conflicted view of sexuality in the region.

Clearly related to a pathological exaggeration in some families of this regional sexual conflict, we have felt from our clinical work, is the relatively frequent occurrence of emotional disorders in Eastern Kentucky children and adults based primarily on sexual conflict. We found that sexual conflicts were prominent in those children presenting with the following psychopathological disorders: hysterical, or conversion reactions; hysterical personality disorders (adolescent girls); and various other types of personality disorders (adolescent boys with underlying psychosexual identity problems).

Clinicians and researchers who have studied hysteria in different population groups have sometimes found sources of conflict other than sexuality to be prominent in persons having these disorders. Edwin Weinstein, for example, felt that conflicts over hostile, aggressive impulses were crucial to the development of various conversion reactions in the adult men he studied in an eastern-seaboard Veterans Administration hospital.[4] This would suggest that sexual conflict is probably not a universal etiologic factor in hysteria. Rather, most clinicians view hysteria as primarily a disorder of communication, resulting from the inability of the afflicted person to verbalize his conflicted feelings. The conflicts themselves vary from one individual to another. Our field data support the thesis that sexual conflict, regionally determined, is present in an overwhelming majority of those who develop hysteria in Eastern Kentucky. In another region, sexuality may not be so conflictual, or other themes may be more conflict-laden.

Our findings further suggest that psychopathology based on conflicts over sexual maturation and functioning has a higher incidence among Eastern Kentucky children than among urban children (our test group being children referred to the Child Psychiatry Clinic at the University of Kentucky Medical Center). Many children so afflicted continue to present similar disabilities later in adulthood. The mental disorders based on psychosexual conflict are, therefore, a regionally significant group of problems in both children and adults.

REGIONAL TRAINING IN COMMUNICATION PROBLEMS

I have already pointed out how frequently verbal communication is a problem among families in Eastern Kentucky, and certain hypotheses concerning this regional nonverbality were advanced. Related to a pathological exaggeration in some families of this regional verbal conflict, we have felt from our clinical work, is the frequent occurrence of emotional disorders in Eastern Kentucky children and adults based wholly or in large part on the afflicted individual's inability to express conflicted feelings in words. We found that nonverbality was prominent in the very large group of children having psychophysiologic and conversion reactions, reactions in which the communication problem is as essential for the development of the disorders as are the underlying dependency or psychosexual conflict themes. Nonverbality was of prime etiologic importance as well in those few children presenting with elective mutism or the consolidated-school syndrome. Overall, these disorders could be viewed primarily as disorders of communication. Beyond our clinical data, school experiences demonstrate the adverse effects of regional nonverbality on the course of the intellectual-cognitive development of many of the children. The combined evidence suggests the thesis that regional nonverbality is a third training theme or pattern of great importance in the total life-adjustive patterns of many Eastern Kentucky children and adults.

These three child-developmental patterns—training in dependency, training in psychosexual conflict, and training in nonverbality—undoubtedly are prominent in the wider Southern Appalachian region as well as in Eastern Kentucky itself, and perhaps are found also throughout the rural South. The joint importance of the three themes as a basis for much of the psychopathology we saw in Eastern Kentucky children over the past six years is underscored by the following figure: roughly 80 percent of all the children we saw in the field clinics during this period came to us with disorders arising from one or more of these three themes.

PROJECTED RESEARCH

A promising basis for related kinds of research would be provided by longitudinal child-development studies in the Southern Appalachian region. With this primary focus, we could examine the forces that shape these children. We could see and evaluate both the mental disorders they develop and the kinds of adaptive ego strengths that emerge. Longitudinal research of this type can verify, discount, or modify the linkages we believe we see between child-development patterns and certain mental disorders.

Although at the moment we feel confident that these linkages are the best hypotheses that can be made on the basis of our considerable clinical data on children from Eastern Kentucky, only future longitudinal studies can provide the kind of validation that would move our developmental theses to the position of established developmental fact. Then, when one knows more conclusively what the facts of child development are in this particular region, with this particular group of people, one will be in a better position to assist—when his help is asked for—in altering those aspects of the child's early development that are not conducive to optimal human growth and development. In addition, the same person so informed by longitudinally established facts of regional child development can be careful not to alter those aspects of the family's structure and functioning that are shown to contribute to the growing child's ego strengths, or adaptive capacities.

The need for longitudinal studies of Southern Appalachian children from birth, or even starting before birth, is reinforced by the fact that retrospective reconstruction of a child's history is often not a very reliable procedure.[5] As clinicians everywhere are, we were heavily dependent on reconstructive histories of the children we reviewed in the field clinics and in our survey of Eastern Kentucky child development. By careful study, in infancy and childhood, of Southern Appalachian children followed through to later life, we could better answer some obvious questions. Certainly we should be able to throw some light on the questions we have raised—whether certain experiences in infancy or early childhood inevitably distort, or on the other hand protect and ensure, the development of various functioning aspects of a healthy personality. In the Southern Appalachian region, as elsewhere, there is a need for more studies of individual human life cycles, beginning, ideally, with the beginning of life.

Two other related areas of research with Southern Appalachian families and their children suggest themselves. First, interdisciplinary studies comparing the life-adjustive patterns of migrant families with the coping capacities and achievements of families that remain in the Southern Appalachian region ought to yield data helpful to city planners, various agency personnel, and others who work with migrant families. Some sociological studies of this type have been done or are underway; none, however, has taken into account the comparative psychopathology involved in family members who later move away from the region.

Second, much-needed epidemiological studies on psychopathology in children from the region have not been made. A study of this type, in an appropriately circumscribed area of the region, would give immediate shape and direction to mental health planning for children, as well as suggest critical areas to be included in longitudinal studies of child development.

PART II   New
                 Paths

CHAPTER 10   New
              Health
              Programs

Ultimately, in Eastern Kentucky as
anywhere else, it is people that make
the area important. It is the people
of the southern mountains, in their
region or in the places to which they
migrate, who are the makers and
carriers of their society and culture.
They are the ones, primarily, who
train the rising generation of their
children and live their lives in either
satisfyingly productive or bleakly nonproductive ways. Thus, although
many agencies, bureaus, and departments of the federal government and
the various state governments are
rightfully concerned with natural-
resource development in Appalachia
and with ways of fostering regional
industrial growth, these concerns must
not become the central ones. Rather,
they must be viewed as they offer
opportunities for people and as they
affect the growth and development
of children.
    Hence this study of family life and
child development in Eastern Kentucky, and of the results of that development in the mental health or
mental disorder of the children, is

finally directed toward opportunities for enhancing the growth of people in the region. For too long the area and the people, with their developmental strengths and weaknesses, have faded in and out of public view. At present there are those within and outside the region who insist that Appalachia rise economically. My request is simply that the personal qualities of the people of the southern mountains, and the forces which shape them, be carefully considered, so that the growth of the people and of their region are taken as inseparably related.

When we consider the difficulties of the people of Appalachia, whether in the mountains or in the cities, it is the manifold problems of the very poor that are the most vexing. The stable working class, the middle and the upper classes in the region generally succeed remarkably well in providing for their health, education, and welfare needs. The most important developmental force accounting for this success is regional familism. By ensuring that even limited resources will be shared among the extended family, particularly at times of crisis, familism stabilizes family life, structure, and functioning. This positive side of familism provides a steady state even for very poor families. In this respect the Appalachian very poor, unlike the frequently socially disorganized very poor families raised in urban slums, possess a strength that can be tapped—as in the case of Danny and his family—for redirection of their lives in many areas. But one nevertheless encounters real problems in attempting to reach the Appalachian very poor with various health, education, and welfare service programs.

BARRIERS TO BE OVERCOME

At the present time, as well as in the past, any number of professionals from a variety of public and private health-care, educational, welfare, and vocational agencies have sought to bring their services to needy Appalachian people, whether these people be generally poor families who continue to live in the region or those who have migrated to urban ghettos. In their attempts to bring their expertise to bear on a particular area of a stricken family's living, these outside professionals have frequently met a solid wall of apathy and resistance from the family itself. The sorely needed service or aid has not been accepted in any real sense of the term. More often this service—a welfare check, for example—has been silently taken and later perhaps misused. Nothing, really, has been exchanged in the transaction except a sum generally inadequate to meet the family's needs for food, clothing, and shelter.

The paradigm holds true in the health-care field. The living conditions of the very poor in Appalachia, their apathy, and the meagerness of resources have often forced medical care into inadequate, symptomatic, crisis-oriented patterns. Nothing has occurred in these encounters of failure—for that is what these abortive attempts to give and receive some sort of aid really are— because people's lives have not been touched. The helping professional feels rebuffed, unwanted, unfulfilled as a helper. The potential recipient of the full measure of his aid, the Appalachian person in need, comes away from such an encounter feeling equally misunderstood and further rejected.

Thomas Ford points up several aspects of this barrier of resistance between the helping person and the family of the Appalachian lower class:

It is extremely difficult for "outside" agencies to reach these [Appalachian] families that most need their help. Community institutions, it has already been noted, are not traditional mechanisms for handling "personal" problems in Appalachia. Numerous studies have documented that poor families do not participate much in community organizations of any type, including the church. And, because the personnel of these institutions are themselves often strangers, they frequently generate even greater insecurities on the part of those they are trying to serve. Dr. Looff's discussion of the "consolidated-school syndrome" provides rather dramatic evidence of how traumatic a new experience can be to children, especially when it must be faced apart from the family. The exaggerated fear of the unfamiliar institution is not confined to children. Stories abound of the very real apprehension and anxiety of adults forced by circumstance to utilize the services of an unfamiliar organization such as a hospital or a government agency office.[1]

The characteristic life-style of the person in the Appalachian lower class—with its trained-in individualism, traditionalism, religious fatalism, action-orientation, and stoicism in manner and speech—works toward an inner-directedness that cuts the person off from community institutions and from cooperative participation with a stranger in meeting, defining, and attempting to solve his problems.

This failure of many of our community institutions to reach the Appalachian poor was painfully demonstrated for me years ago in both the general health-care and the mental health field. In the late 1950s, and again in the early 1960s, I was a trainee in large university-based, community-funded child psychiatry clinics, in Baltimore and in Cincinnati. Both of these children's clinics were conducted in large hospital settings, and both ostensibly served, among many others, families of the Appalachian migrant poor. My experience in both clinics sharply highlighted Ford's remarks. Migrant families were referred in great numbers to these agencies, but a majority of them did not return after meeting the large, strange staff in the unfamiliar setting and after encountering insistence on regular appointments for their succeeding visits. Too often, I feel now, these clinics—like many other community institutions that try to reach the Appalachian poor—took the position that their responsibility ended when the families had demonstrated low motivation for self-help by failing to return for care. Clinic services were available only on a take-it-or-leave-it basis. The customary rationalization of this position was that the clinics simply had insufficient staff to do otherwise. In one clinic, personnel were acutely aware of their failure to meet the needs of the Appalachian migrant poor but were at a loss as to how to break through these barriers of apparent apathy or resistance.

The initial point at which these health-care agencies failed in delivering services to Appalachian migrant families was their lack of understanding of the life-style of these families. The personal orientation of the mountaineer steeped in familism makes it very difficult—virtually impossible at first—for him to relate to total strangers in unfamiliar agency settings. In addition, his aversion to routines and to the agency's time-oriented casework schedules generally guarantees that he will not cooperate with the agency. This raises the question as to whether the particular life-style of the person in the Appalachian lower class forever precludes his receiving help from various community institutions.

I think not, on the basis of my own sharply contrasting experiences in helping to deliver one type of health service to Appalachian families. My earlier experience, in Baltimore and Cincinnati, was one of sharing many failures with my colleagues in the urban agencies. However, the experiences I have had in helping many families and their children through the Manchester Project have forever erased from my mind any doubts that all kinds of health services can be brought effectively to Appalachian families. The essential difference between my experiences of clinical failure, on the one hand, and clinical success, on the other, is not, I feel, any factor that resides in me as a person or as a child psychiatrist. Rather, the essential difference that spelled success in the Manchester Project was the different point of view of this work itself. It took squarely into account the fact that Appalachian people are person oriented; their characteristic trait of orientation to self, the intimate, the personal proved to be the point at which community agencies can begin to relate to them.

It will be recalled that the Manchester Project was originally formulated by persons in the region—the county health officer and her staff of senior public health nurses—who were well acquainted with the families they served and, in turn, were accepted by these families as familiar givers of aid. The sub-culture-based empathy of the nurses was the prime factor in the establishment of our mental health work in the familiar setting of the local health departments, in the constant utilization of the diagnostic-treatment services of the nurses in direct mental health work with families, and in the regular use of nurses in our consultations with schools and community agencies. We literally did not plan or make a move without the assistance of the familiar, accepted public health nurse.

In time we, too—the other members of the project's clinic teams, who were the "outsiders"—came to be accepted by the families we served. The relative success of the Manchester Project in meeting many of the mental health needs of a substantial number of Eastern Kentucky children and their families unquestionably demonstrates the effectiveness of planning for "personalization of services" for Appalachian families. Obviously, mental health services or even general health services are not the only kinds of services needed by these families. They have a host of inadequacies, calling for educational, welfare, vocational, and recreational services. The ultimate success or failure of the various agencies in delivering these services to the Appalachian poor depends upon the extent to which each agency can personalize its approach. Jack Weller also underscores this central point, namely that the utilization of a personal approach is essential for agencies working with Appalachian families whose value systems stress the intimate and the personal.[2]

SUGGESTIONS FOR GENERAL HEALTH SERVICES

Just how this personalization of services is to be accomplished by various community agencies serving the Appalachian poor merits some discussion. First of all, the pronounced fear of illness shared by Appalachian families of all socioeconomic classes, based as it is on the threat to the family's solidarity, is one factor leading toward their acceptance of any health-care service. And it is certainly true that achieving better health for all family members is a crucial early step in the family's efforts to master the tasks confronting it.

The second consideration involves planning a health service, regardless of the type, around familiar givers of aid in a familiar setting. If the service can be organized in this manner, it is more likely to reach the families it hopes to serve. For example, I feel that a well-baby, prenatal, mental-health or other type of field clinic designed to meet the needs of the Appalachian migrant poor in a large city should be based in the migrants' community. We are well aware, from the work of several rural sociologists,[3] how Appalachian families migrate to and from little neighborhood pockets of their kinsmen and friends within large cities. It would be essential, then, for the planned health service to fit into this pattern—to locate within the migrant community in a building that is itself quite familiar to families in the area.

It would be equally essential for the health service to utilize as the prime givers of aid those persons to whom the families in the area naturally turn for talk and counsel. In Eastern Kentucky, people have this relationship with the public health nurses in the local health departments. This might not be true in large urban settings, where the public health nurse may be just another outsider. If so, then a search must be made to discover just who it is that migrant families accept and relate to. It may be several of their number, generally women, who serve as informal but effective community leaders. These people should be employed as the ones who refer families to the health service, get them to come, and encourage them to continue. Their role in this work would be to bridge the emotional or resistance gap between the Appalachian families and the health-care professionals. A prototype of such a person exists in the form of the home aides who are now functioning as bridges between the enrichment classrooms for very poor preschool children and their homes in ten Eastern Kentucky counties.

One of these home aides, Mrs. Ora Gibson, whose family has lived for several generations in Owsley County, demonstrated for me several years ago just how effective a catalyst role such a local woman can play. A great yarn-spinner, Mrs. Gibson told me the story of one particular family she had helped. These people, the Ocie Carters, lived on a partially timbered hillside at the very end of their hollow. The wife, Mattie, an extremely shy, reclusive woman of thirty-eight, seldom left the place; she spent her time tilling the garden, carrying water for cooking and washing from the creek, and attempting to keep up with the demands of her six wild children, who ranged in ages from four to twelve. Ocie, forty-two, had worked for some years in the mines and drew a small pension for black-lung disability. This pension would have been adequate to feed and clothe his family, but Ocie shared with some of his men cronies in the area a strong liking for pedigreed coon hounds and for gambling. The money went in those directions instead of to the family. The children ran barefoot in all kinds of weather, were poorly fed and clothed, and consequently were frequently seen as sickly by the public health department. Mattie never raised her voice in protest when Ocie bought the six rolls of half-inch, heavy-duty chicken wire for a new pen for his dogs or bought another used car to make a trip to central Indiana to buy an expensive new coon dog. Ocie fed his dogs a well-balanced diet of fairly expensive dry meal, and he bought a new shotgun to hunt with them. When not hunting or riding around with his cronies, he was gambling or cussing his kids—who attended school only when they wanted to, which was infrequent.

Ocie's behavior and lack of attention to the obvious needs of his wife and children had drawn down community anger and frustration upon him. School officials tried in vain to reason with him about his children's need for education and to impress upon him how he could help them by sending them to school regularly. Public health officials were appalled at the neglect of the children's health needs. But their efforts to reach Ocie were likewise ineffectual. The public-assistance worker and a local minister had also talked with Ocie about his need to change his ways, again to no avail. Everyone in the community had given up on the man. "He's just stupid and no count!" seemed to be the general feeling.

A year later, Ocie's youngest boy, Sam, reached the age of four and became eligible for the Owsley County day-care program. When the boy began to attend, Mrs. Ora Gibson was assigned to the Carters as a home aid. She, like the other aides, had only general instructions to "go on in there, see what the home's like, and do what you can to help."

As Mrs. Gibson told me later, her initial visits with the Carters were altogether different in approach from those of other community-agency workers. "I got up in that holler late one day after the longest walk. Car just wouldn't go any farther on that dry creek bed. I was thirsty, too, when I got there and Mattie said she ain't got no fresh water yet—it's still down in the creek. But she didn't send no young'uns for it—and they was plenty of them running around, I tell you. Ocie, he just grinned and looked at me and said the only water he knew about up at the house was over in the dog's pen. Right then and there I see right off what shape things be in. I figger Ocie's stuck on them dogs and nuthin' else. So I decided to play it his way for a while. I said I'd sure like to see them dogs, and before another minute went by Ocie took me up to the pen. The two dogs he had were real pretty ones, especially the bitch from Indiana. And I told him so—they *were* nice dogs. I like dogs as much as anybody, I guess, maybe more sometimes. And these were so friendly. I patted 'em, and Ocie was so pleased he let me open the pen and take 'em out. We walked 'em around until it was time for me to go. I told Ocie I'd be back to see him the end of the week, and he grinned and said 'Come any time!' He meant it, too, 'cause on Friday when I came back we took the dogs on a hunt in the woods—just Ocie and me. Plumb tuckered me, scramblin' over logs and in and out of swales, but I kinda liked it all, and Ocie sure did, I could tell that."

Three weeks apparently passed in a similar manner. On each of her twice-weekly home visits, Mrs. Gibson spoke initially only with Ocie and then spent her time entirely with him and his beloved dogs.

One day during the fourth week, as Mrs. Gibson related it to me, "we had a real gully-washer of a rain. I could see the dog pen saggin' all over the place in that-there soft dirt. Ocie, he grinned and took me up there again. Made me mad—all that good chicken-wire goin' to waste, saggin' down and fallin' down, and them pretty dogs havin' no decent place now. And I told Ocie so—I didn't care. I told him to fetch me a shovel, and he says, 'Miz Gibson, what you fixin' to do with it? You look mad enough to clobber me with it right off!' I told him I was mad all right, but I wasn't gonna hit him yet, if he helped me shovel out the new post holes to set that-there fence up right again. The idea, lettin' a thing like that go to rack and ruin! Makes a body mad! So we worked up there all afternoon. Tough it was, and ever' time Ocie wanted to lay off and rest a spell I told him the next shovelful from me was for him. I told him it was a bald-faced shame to care for them pretty dogs so bad, that they had as much right as him or me to have a decent pen.

"The next time I come up there Ocie looked downright shame-faced, if I ever did see a man look like that. He come up to me and he sez, 'Miz Gibson, you shamed me right. I guess I don't take care of nuthin' much.' Then Ocie told me he had sold the male dog to Ned Scroggins and kept the bitch. He figured, he told me, that he wasn't doin' any better by Mattie and the young 'uns then with that dog pen, so he took the extra money he got and took them all to town for shoes and a picture show. And Ocie told me, 'Miz Gibson, I'm gonna make us both proud,' and he did. I told him that any man who could shovel a post hole the way he done could go on the road gang [the OEO-funded Work Experience and Training Program] in the county, and he went." From that point on, there began to be evidence of better functioning in the Carter family.

Mrs. Gibson, unknowingly but in a natural, intuitive manner, had apparently followed the casework principle of helping a person overcome his adaptive weaknesses by working supportively with him from a position of his manifest strengths. Unlike Mrs. Gibson, earlier community workers, in effect, had assailed Ocie for his weaknesses. This only increased his defensiveness and reinforced his indifference to his family's needs. Mrs. Gibson, however, was genuinely fond of dogs, which gave her an immediate bond of rapport with Mr. Carter, whose dog care was his principal interest and strength at the moment. As a consequence of strengthening this bond by working with Ocie around his interests and supporting him in them, Mrs. Gibson found later that the man was receptive to her confrontation over his lapse in care. Ocie himself made the application to his family, when he felt genuinely liked and supported and was consequently less defensive.

Mrs. Gibson's story is a very good basic demonstration of the effective way a local person can relate to poor families and assist them with a variety of tasks and problems. It is a person like her I have in mind as the bridge between various community programs and the people these programs are designed to serve. Further, the type of assistance rendered by Mrs. Gibson demonstrates again how effective frequent home visits by the bridging person can be, both in leading to a clear understanding of a given family's weaknesses and strengths ("Right then and there I see right off what shape things be in") and in providing the most natural opportunities to work with others. These frequent home visits tend to reinforce the personal approach needed for a family's acceptance of a helper's suggestions or an agency's program. This home visiting was a highly effective technique in the Manchester Project. Many times I have had the profoundly gratifying experience of finding my mental health recommendations better accepted on the family's front porch over a cup of their coffee than in my office across my desk.

SUGGESTIONS FOR MENTAL HEALTH SERVICES

Thus far, suggested outlines for the organization and the delivery of general health-care services to very poor Appalachian families have been drawn from our experience in the Manchester Project. These considerations are equally essential, I feel, to the conduct of local or even regional mental health-mental retardation services for Appalachian adults and children. I am suggesting, in effect, that our experience in the project can serve as a demonstration leading to the development of new mental health services for those living in rural Appalachia and for migrant families in the cities.

I feel that it is important to establish any new mental health services for Appalachian children within already established general health clinics. As I have said, Appalachian families are accustomed to gravitating to one setting for all their health needs. The setting itself has grown familiar to them, as well as the people who staff the agency. In addition, there is much to recommend the inclusion of the home health aides in mental health work as well as general health work. The unique vantage point provided by their frequent home visits enables these aides to serve as monitors of the early development of the children in the families they serve. When they report on developmental lags and problems, early case intervention can be accomplished. You will remember that the Eastern Kentucky public health nurses, by checking frequently on the development of children in their districts, were in a prime position to help families redirect various features of the children's training if change were needed and to make early referrals to our mental health clinics if further evaluation and treatment services were required.

Aside from these general considerations, common to both general health-care and mental health services, two further factors, I feel, have important implications specifically for the mental health area. Both are drawn from our experience in the Manchester Project.

The first is that our project had a continual shortage of qualified psychiatric personnel. Even though the program was established, organized, and greatly extended by the public health nurses, we simply were not able to reach every family in these four Eastern Kentucky counties that needed mental health services for their children. Knowing that this would undoubtedly be true as our work continued, we planned from the outset to extend our mental health reach even further by providing regular case consultations to the Head Start and day-care programs, to the schools, and to public-assistance and other agencies caring for children. The consultation program, which was a supplement to our direct therapeutic work with families, was designed to contribute to the effectiveness of these other community insituations that were seeking to help the people in other ways. For example, we as consultants attempted to help the staffs of these agencies gain a better understanding of the severe emotional stresses faced by people who are very poor in the area, of some of the behavioral consequences of these severe and chronic stresses.

Sometimes we were able to point out the additional stresses which agency personnel themselves, however unwittingly, placed particularly on the very poor, and we discussed the need to eliminate these tensions before the workers could render their intended services. We sometimes encountered stress of this type resulting from the expression of overtly negative views toward members of the Appalachian lower class. Other agency workers sometimes held covertly negative attitudes that produced therapeutic apathy, rather than attitudes recognizing the potential for change in the lower class. Such attitudes, when continued, blocked the building of security and confidence, which must exist in order to establish and maintain a service relationship between agency personnel and clients.

We felt that the negativism on the part of agency people, when it was found, was based on the familiar conflict over class identity known to sociologists and others who have studied various disadvantaged or minority groups. Those few agency staff members who reacted negatively to the poor in the region were reacting, I feel, to a threatened loss of their own hard-won middle-class, professional identity. At times they were made anxious by the public pronouncements of outsiders who threatened to blur class boundaries and to identify them with the Appalachian lower class. This accounted for the anger that many middle-class residents of the area felt toward Walter Cronkite's special broadcast, which seemed to them to deal solely with the local lower class. At other times, the middle-class professional person who attempted to assist a person of the lower class was made similarly frustrated and angry by what he felt was the poor person's calculated resistance to change. "I made it out of poverty—why can't he? He's just lazy and stupid!" was one way of expressing these attitudes. For other professional people, such direct angry acting-out of feelings toward those in the lower class was intolerable; these people instead internalized the anxiety-laden conflict based on class identity. The therapeutic apathy and nihilistic attitudes that subsequently developed prevented the effective working together of the helping person and his client. Our further role in the consultation program was to assist in identifying these feelings, if they existed in members of agencies serving families in the area, and to attempt to bring the feelings out into the open for discussion and resolution.

Our experience produces a second consideration that is highly important here. It has to do with the place of psychotherapy and social casework in the treatment of Appalachian families. More specifically, it concerns whether we have found that these verbal techniques have any merit in the treatment of the Appalachian poor.

I raise this point because at one time there existed in the nation the widely prevalent opinion that psychotherapy is neither the treatment of choice nor an effective treatment at all for very poor or even working-class people. Past failures of psychotherapy with some low-income groups in certain parts of the country, it is true, may have been largely due to the insistence there on reconstructive, insight-oriented treatment of the kind long in use with the middle and upper classes. Several studies have documented the failure of such static forms of treatment to reach the poor.[4] However, our experience in the Manchester Project clearly indicates that many poor Appalachian families are able to express feelings and ideas sensitively in words and therefore represent a group that can make effective use of insight-directed, even long-term psychotherapy and casework. These families exist side by side with other low-income, "non-verbal" families, for whom, I would agree, revised, action-oriented, crisis-model approaches seem more appropriate. Our conclusion is that the approach in mental health treatment must be flexible and fitted to the values, attitudes, and needs of the families being served.

I should also say that, while individual psychotherapy is certainly no substitute for correction of the noxious social conditions that afflict the low-income people of the southern mountains, it is also true that environmental measures alone may fail to alleviate symptoms of personality disorder based on internal emotional problems. Internal problems, as well as external stresses, may contribute to the particular distress of the very poor in Appalachia. Comprehensive planning to assist families of all income groups in the area must of necessity, therefore, take both internal and external sources of stress into consideration.

CHAPTER 11   New
Community
Programs

In the course of our clinical study of
Eastern Kentucky families we talked
with many different people—teachers,
ministers, physicians, public-assistance
and child welfare workers, and others.
At first, these conferences were designed to round out our understanding
of the problems or progress of particular children we were reviewing at
the moment in our field clinics. Later,
a regular program of case consultation
to the schools and agencies in the
counties served by our project afforded us the opportunity of exploring
together the effects these community
institutions had on the developing
lives of children. We came to understand something about the schools and
agencies themselves—the joys and
burdens of the teachers and caseworkers who daily came into contact
with the children. From these conferences and talks over the years, I
have formed certain impressions about
the strengths and weaknesses of these
institutions outside the family.

My impressions are presented here
as lines of action that Southern Appalachian communities might follow

in order to enhance the overall development of their children. In making these formulations I am mindful of three factors. First, I have generalized from my experiences in Eastern Kentucky to comment on the wider Southern Appalachian region. Second, the suggestions I make about changed policies for program development are in many instances not uniquely my own; generally they were first formulated by persons in the various community institutions, who really have the inside track when it comes to perceiving the impact of the region and its institutions on growing children.

The third factor concerns the critical importance of all types of community institutions themselves in helping to shape the lives of these children. In urban, middle-class America it is the nuclear, or immediate, family that is of transcendent importance in the rearing of children; community institutions simply extend the family's training influence by reinforcing what is being taught at home. Today this pattern holds true for the Southern Appalachian middle and upper classes. But when we consider the Southern Appalachian lower class—the very poor, and the poor yet stable working-class families—we face the problem of large gaps in family training of children. These training deficits create some of the particular kinds of problems afflicting the children described in this book. I do not think we can expect Southern Appalachian lower-class families, by themselves, to identify and remedy these training gaps. Instead, these families will need much continuing personal support from several kinds of community institutions. Many others feel as I do on this point. Thomas Ford not only has this same view but also suggests a broad outline for a community approach to this problem:

It is my contention that the traditional family mechanisms have not been adequate to solve the problems of the poor in Appalachia or elsewhere in our modern society. *Increasingly some of the burden must be shifted to other institutional systems.* Before this can be done, however, the institutions must be able to reach the families, which thus far they [often] have not done very successfully. A two-pronged approach to the establishment of relations would appear to be in order. One approach would be to work directly with the families, helping them to function more adequately. The second approach would be to work with community institutions, aiding their personnel to gain a more sympathetic understanding of the [lower class] families they must serve. In my judgment, psychiatry has a great deal to offer to both approaches if we expand the psychiatric perspective of poverty to include not only the poor but also those who seek to assist them.[1]

Here again, as in my suggestions for general and mental health programs, my primary concern is for the Appalachian lower class. As I talk about various community institutions, it is the training needs of the children of the poor that remain in focus.

The past decade has seen considerable national support for—and research on—the supplemental training of preschool children who are poor. The federally and state-subsidized day-care nurseries and Head Start programs are well-known examples. Eastern Kentucky has shared this interest in several ways.

Each of the four counties served by the Manchester Project has for the past several summers conducted a Head Start program for late preschool children. The format of each program has been similar to those of programs elsewhere. Half-day classes are held in churches or elementary schools, usually in the county seat, for a six- to eight-week period. Local elementary teachers, assisted by housewives as classroom aides, provide the instruction. Because of the inadequacy of funds for materials and staff, classes are never large enough to provide a place for every eligible child in these rural mountain counties. Attendance is on an elective basis; parents decide whether or not they wish their child to attend. The result is hardly surprising: the experience of each of the four county-school systems has been that many more working- and middle-class than lower-class children participate.

Local elementary teachers feel that several factors operate together to account for the relative failure of Head Start to reach the children who most sorely need a supplemental enrichment program. First is the difficulty of telling far-flung poor families in all the hollows that such classes exist. Even so, many poor families who have been informed remain reluctant to send their child to classes "so far 'way from home." The characteristic inner-directedness of lower-class families, with their great need to cling to one another and to avoid separation of family members, undergirds this reluctance. One working-class father I know pinpointed this phenomenon when he expressed his reluctance to send two of his preschool daughters to the University of Kentucky Medical Center for needed clinical work: "Doc, there just ain't nobody goin' to spearmint on my babies!"

Furthermore, the marginally funded Head Start programs lack the money often to employ local people who, in the capacity of home aides, could possibly counteract this particular reluctance by bridging the emotional gulf that parents put between themselves and school. Most local teachers feel firmly that lower-class children in the region will not attend Head Start—or any other school program, for that matter—on a regular, continuing basis until this kind of personal support is given to their parents. It takes time and money to meet with lower-class parents in their homes, to win their acceptance, and with this acceptance to gain their willingness to send their children to the "strange program." But without this kind of supported redirection, Head Start in the region will continue to fall far short of its intended goal.

COMMUNITY DAY-CARE PROGRAMS

In contrast to regional Head Start, which has often failed to reach the children of the poor, two types of community day-care programs exclusively for four-year-olds from poor families have recently been established in parts of Eastern Kentucky. The Rural Child Care Project, supported by federal and state funds through the Kentucky Department of Child Welfare, has for several years conducted experimental day-care programs in ten of the thirty-two Eastern Kentucky counties. Two of the four counties served by our field clinics have participated in the project. Along with several other psychiatrists and social workers, I have served as a part-time consultant.

Those who are eligible for day care are the four-year-olds of families on public assistance. Participation is on an elective, first-come-first-served basis. At the present level of funded support, approximately eighty children can be included in each county's program each year; this figure represents perhaps 10 to 20 percent of eligible poor children in each county.

The other day-care project is one recently funded under the OEO-sponsored community action program in Clay County, one of the four counties served by our field clinics. The two separate day-care projects are similar in staff and programs.

Each day-care program is housed in an old elementary school building. Classes are held Mondays through Fridays throughout the year from 8:00 A.M. to 3:00 P.M. The children are bussed in from throughout the county. The elementary teachers and the aides conduct classes. Other local housewives serve as home aides to the families whose children are in school (but, again, not to families who *could* have children in school).

Instruction of the children is of a generally high caliber. A wide range of excellent teaching materials appropriate for the perceptual-cognitive development of preschool children is provided for each program. In addition to regular kindergarten instruction, there is considerable planned participation by these previously isolated children in group social activities. Attention is given in group interaction to the development of speech and to language as an effective social tool. Field trips are taken beyond the mountain counties to industries, the state capitol, zoos, and parks.

During the time the children are in school, the home aides meet with parents in their homes to interpret the programs the children are undertaking. The aides also attempt to reinforce the children's instruction by helping the parents to establish and maintain adequate diets and standards of cleanliness, to understand the importance of a balance between need gratification and the setting of limits for their children, and to set and maintain appropriate disciplinary controls. After they have formed personal relationships with these families, the aides are generally accepted in their role. In effect, they do whatever they feel is necessary at the moment to help these parents guide their children.

Empirical observations by program administrators, by our consulting staff, and by the elementary teachers in the lower-grade classes to which these children had gone following their year's training in day care indicate the overall effectiveness of the programs in aiding the personality-emotional-intellectual development of many of these poor preschool children. The children are generally cleaner and better fed. For the most part they are happier, more alert, and curious. Compared with children who have not been in day care, far fewer of them have intense separation concerns on entering the first grade. Language skills of the day-care children are improved, and their group social skills have been broadened. Elementary teachers have also observed that the day-care children read more fluently, with greater comprehension, than do their untrained peers. Current plans call for examination of these observations through follow-up psychometric testing of the children, to measure both their gains in personal-social skills and their progress in perceptual-cognitive development. The homelife of the families, after a year of association with the home aides, has generally improved as well. The types of changes that have been noted in these families parallel the progress made by Danny's family, described earlier.

The experimental regional day-care programs for lower-class preschool children have, in my opinion as well as in that of the administrators and of other consultants, sufficiently established their effectiveness with many Eastern Kentucky families to warrant a high-priority recommendation: similar programs should be funded to include all the eligible Southern Appalachian poor.

REGIONAL EDUCATIONAL VOCATIONAL TRAINING PROGRAMS

The trend in education in Eastern Kentucky over the past decade has been toward the establishment of consolidated schools at the elementary, junior high, and senior high levels. Each year, more and more one-, two-, and three-room schools in neighborhood coves and hollows are being closed. Some of the counties have now achieved their goal of total school consolidation. Others, like Clay County, expect to reach this point within the next few years. With consolidation has come, generally, gradual improvement in the quality of teaching materials and nearly all the teachers are now college graduates. Inevitably, the children themselves have gained a broader view of the world through participation with a wider group of their peers. And, finally, consolidation has made possible increasing numbers of special educational classes for the mentally retarded and the neurologically handicapped.

But consolidation has also brought into sharp focus very real problems of the region's children. Classes are mixed; that is, children of all three socioeconomic groups are put together by grade and age. They are not generally grouped by measured skills or achievement levels. Thus, one frequently finds culturally disadvantaged, slow-learning, often infrequently attending boys and girls of the lower class grouped together with working-class, middle-class, and upper-class children who are for the most part achieving at their grade levels. Given such a mixed class of perhaps thirty-six pupils, an elementary teacher is often frustrated. Classes are too large, generally, to permit the teachers to give the many slower students the individual instruction they obviously need. To do this adequately would take all the teachers' time and the students working at grade level would suffer in the process. Accordingly, this conflict has been solved by many of the teachers in the direction of teaching at grade level. As a consequence, many lower-class children in Eastern Kentucky elementary schools, almost as a standard procedure, repeat each grade once and then are "socially promoted." Others are socially promoted on a yearly basis. As many of these lower-class children reach preadolescence and their early adolescent years—if not before—the long years of continual educational failure and frustration catch·up with them. They drop out of school to idle around home, to drift about the local community, or to migrate eventually to a city. In no way under such an educational system have very many of these lower-class children been trained in any skills that are marketable—or even that promote self-esteem. Consequently, most of them inevitably join the ranks of the unemployed.

Recently, in a partial attempt to meet the training needs of this large, unschooled group of older adolescents and young adults in Eastern Kentucky, regional vocational schools have been established. Entrance requirements are stringent: a boy or young adult must have at least a tenth-grade education and, if he is currently enrolled in a high school, must be performing satisfactorily in his studies. These new vocational schools are meeting the needs of a portion of the area's young adult population. But, on the other hand, a majority of lower-class, and many working-class children—the ones who most sorely need trade training—drop out of school long before the tenth grade and remain, therefore, forever ineligible for regional vocational training as it is now being conducted.

One day, three fourth-grade teachers in one of the con- solidated elementary schools spoke to me with great feeling about this regional training dilemma and also about a possible solution. One of them summed things up: "Doctor Looff, what are we going to do with these twelve-thirteen-fourteen-year-olds who are still in our fourth-grade classes? They can't learn from books and they don't come to class regularly. But they are really very likable kids, and they're smart enough. Some of them know a great deal about the woods, animals, streams, and hunting and fishing. Their families are dirt-poor and really don't hold to book learning. These kids know that—they don't hold to it either—and they get meaner the longer they go on failing in their lessons. We think we need two kinds of fourth grades: the kind we teach now for most of the children and a special kind for these others."

I can firmly agree with what these fourth-grade teachers were saying to me. There is indeed a need in Eastern Kentucky for vocational training of many children of the lower socioeconomic class, and it should begin early in the lower elementary grades. I do not want to be misunderstood on this point. It has nothing whatever to do with class structure as such. It is based on the fact that these children have received their early perceptual-cognitive training in concrete operations, action-oriented toward performance tasks rather than toward the use of numbers and words as abstract symbols. The introduction of task-oriented trade training early in their school years would meet the expectations these children have for themselves. The lower-class child who is proud of his skills in making a whistle in the spring from a slippery-willow switch ought to be similarly gratified in time by his gradual mastery of the kinds of performance skills required, for example, in carpentry. But if the crucial early years of his schooling—years that normally involve a certain level of curiosity, initiative, and pleasure in the mastery of various learning tasks—continue to be invalidated for the lower-class child by attempts to train him solely in abstract operations, he will undoubtedly continue to develop into the nonproductive dropout from school.

In such a redirection of training for many younger lower-class and working-class children, careful consideration would have to be given to the actual graded content of such a program, to the formulation of criteria by which children are selected for trade child in the program, and to interlocking the elementary trades training, to provisions for follow-up or tracking of a particular program with advanced vocational training.

REGIONAL PUBLIC ASSISTANCE PROGRAMS

In Eastern Kentucky, as elsewhere in the nation, the present public-assistance program has been relatively ineffective in accomplishing its original goal of providing financial support to families only until the time they are again economically productive and able to sustain themselves. Several factors contribute to the weakness of the program. First, the traditional individualism of the mountaineer, with its self-oriented value system, tends to lead a family to accept public welfare as their due. A second and perhaps more important factor is the fact that under present law public welfare support is oriented toward the husbandless woman and her dependent children. Some women in the mountains have indeed lost their husbands through death, divorce, or final desertion and consequently stand in need of temporary financial support. In many other Eastern Kentucky families, however, the lack of available work in the area leads men to desert their families temporarily in order to render them eligible for financial aid. In the process, however, the family loses the necessary emotional support of the husband and father. The frequency of this pattern of planned desertion has led some familiar with public-assistance programs in Eastern Kentucky to refer to the phenomenon as "the absent-father syndrome" (although this pattern is, of course, not confined to Eastern Kentucky or to Appalachia).

Several children referred to our field clinics have had behavioral symptoms based on sadness, anxieties, and anger related to this kind of absence of their fathers. In addition, the training model presented to the children is of male inadequacy in role performance. "Daddy is worth something to Mommy when he is gone," was the devastating comment one sad but perceptive child made to me.

In the interest of furthering a more normal pattern of family life, structure, and functioning, public-assistance laws and directives now being proposed should be reoriented toward the financial support of the man with his family. What this man really needs is help for the period of time required for other agencies to train him in a marketable skill and to assist him in finding work.

REGIONAL WORK PROGRAMS

The economic problems of the Southern Appalachian region at times have seemed insurmountable. On top of the chronic economic deprivation of the area there has gradually developed in many mountain men a combination of exhaustion, fear, pessimism, and defeat, which has served to destroy their self-esteem and ambition and to preclude opportunities for escape. These economic facts and these feelings, taken together as a self-perpetuating cycle of poverty, are reinforced by the region's geographic and cultural isolation, the men's lack of education, and the many special health hazards and problems that confront them and their families.

In the face of these vast and complex problems, the progress made by Danny's family came to us as a real ray of hope. I am suggesting here that this particular family's story be considered as an action model both for the discharge of our social responsibility to the Appalachian poor and for an actual approach to the many problems involved.

Certain salient themes marked the progress of Danny's family. First, the traditional person orientation of the Appalachian mountaineer was the basis of our establishing and maintaining an abiding relationship with the family, a relationship within which, in time, many approaches to the solving of problems were worked out. Second, Virgil, the father, retained a vestige of work-oriented pride that grew into his eventual participation in the "Happy Pappy" work program in his county and also into the firm reestablishment of his own self-esteem. The remainder of their progress, now a matter of firm record, proceeded from these two initial strengths the family possessed and from our therapeutic approaches that were based upon them.

The kind of progress this family made can, I feel, be repeated elsewhere in the mountains and in urban areas with migrant families. Two factors seem to be essential for this progress. First, a person must relate with the family and gradually communicate hope to them over a long period of time. Second, real-work programs must be available in the area. Everything else proceeds from these basic considerations.

The form and quality of real-work programs that are most acceptable to southern mountain men merits some consideration. Many of these men would become soon disenchanted with and drift away from the typical time-oriented, scheduled-by-shift, impersonal orientation of the typical large factory. We already have abundant evidence for this in the work-performance records of many Appalachian migrant men.

Better suited to their life-style is the type of work that involves more flexible schedules, that is action oriented toward performance skills, and above all, that remains person oriented. The Appalachian man's individualism and person orientation suit him for a variety of jobs requiring independent personal services, such as small independent businesses and trades. The intense person orientation of Southern Appalachian men and women should remain, I feel, a prime factor in any local rural, regional, or urban planning for economic development. Planning for many small businesses or individual ancillary trades would constitute a "best fit" with the Appalachian man's trait of personalizing services.

In providing the Southern Appalachian man who is poor with personal support, training, and in work for which he is psychologically best fitted, and in providing redirections in health, education, and welfare programs that touch his life, we shall provide as well for his wife and for his children, in ways that statistics cannot show.

PART III   Backgrounds

CHAPTER 12   The
Region
and Its
People

The Southern Appalachian region, running from West Virginia and part of southeastern Ohio in the north to sections of northern Georgia and Alabama in the south, is a diverse land of mountains, broad river valleys, and eroded highland plateaus. The thirty-two counties that make up Eastern Kentucky are included in the western division of the region, called the Cumberland Plateau. Little of Eastern Kentucky is truly mountainous. The worn, stream-dissected highlands of the Cumberland Plateau present today a remarkably even appearance to one who flies over the region and views it in broad perspective. An aerial view shows how thinly populated the area is, relatively speaking. The impression one gets is of a few tortuous roads that follow the many stream valleys, scattered small towns, isolated farmsteads, and an even, covering blanket of second-growth deciduous woodlands. Here and there one sees a limestone ledge outcropping or an occasional strip coal mine lying like a scar on the land.

Everywhere today, Eastern Kentucky bears the marks of long-standing extractive industries. Coal tipples, some abandoned and derelict, many still in active use, dot the roadsides at the heads of valleys or stand at the edge of many small towns. The coal trucks they load, together with school buses, make up the bulk of the early-morning and late-afternoon traffic on local main roads. Here and there a small sawmill, supporting perhaps no more than a dozen men, roughs out lumber from second-growth oak, hickory, ash, and poplar. Aside from the tipples and mills, the hills and hollows of Eastern Kentucky beyond the few major towns contain no evidence of major industrialization. Instead, small family-owned businesses are scattered along the few main roads in the area—groceries, garages, and an occasional restaurant.

Outside the towns, the people of Eastern Kentucky today still live on the land. A few relatively prosperous farms, rich bottomland in broad stream valleys, support dairy or beef herds as well as annual cash crops of hay, grain, and tobacco. But these farms stand in sharp contrast to the many neighboring hillside clearings, shacks, outhouses, and collective refuse of the stark lives of the very poor in the area. Near them, strung out along the same main roads, are the small subsistence farms of the region's working class, who diligently scratch out their living from the soil, raise a small patch of tobacco as their only annual cash crop, work in the mines and mills, and drive the school buses.

The county seat, a town with a population varying from several hundred to about two thousand, is still the center of today's Eastern Kentucky trading, politics, health-care services, and quiet family visiting. The life of these rural towns is perhaps like that of rural small towns anywhere. Everyone knows everyone else and knows his affairs. Men cluster about the courthouse on court day to visit, to swap yarns, and to argue. Women shop. Lines of the very poor queue up outside distribution centers to receive government surplus food on commodity days. Everyone meets frequently at restaurants like "The Purple Cow" or the "Busy Bee" for sitting and talking, and for pie and coffee. Talk centers on local, largely Republican politics, fall tobacco prices in Lexington or Winchester, family life, and the progress of the local high school basketball team. The elected county judge, who is the county's chief administrative officer, and the school-board-appointed county school superintendent are the two most powerful people in the county. They govern much of its affairs through leadership roles in politics, through control of public moneys, and, frequently and classically, through job patronage. Much local talk centers on these people.

DEMOGRAPHIC FIGURES

The people living in Eastern Kentucky today are by no means socially homogeneous. The area contains a middle class of teachers, shopkeepers, clerks, and farmers as well as a professional and upper class. These classes have much the same characteristics as similar classes anywhere else in the United States. Many serve as community leaders and are considerably ahead of the rest of the population in education, income, and property ownership. Rupert Vance describes them as activists and progessives, receptive to national values and contacts, and definitely ahead of the rank and file of people in advocating change and development in contrast with the local lower class.[1]

Thomas Ford, a sociologist at the University of Kentucky, comments on the economic life chances of people in Eastern Kentucky in his recent book which summarizes much pertinent demographic data for this area.[2]

A suitable index area for a review of this data is Clay County, the largest of the four counties in Eastern Kentucky served by the Manchester Project. Of Clay County's 23,000 population, 2,000 reside in Manchester, the county seat; the remainder of the population is classified as rural farm, or rural nonfarm. Typical as well of other Eastern Kentucky counties, Clay County's percentage of Negro population in 1960 was approximately 1.1 percent of the total. During the decade 1950-1960, Clay County was one of twenty-three counties in Eastern Kentucky having losses amounting to 30 percent or more of their 1950 population. During the same decade the birth rate was thirty and over per 1,000 population, a high rate shared by only three of Kentucky's 120 counties. The death rate, however, did not vary greatly from the national rate. The conclusion is that total population losses were by emigration. This loss trend is not a new one for Kentucky or Clay County, but has persisted throughout the twentieth century in Eastern Kentucky counties whose economies in the past were heavily dependent upon coal mining.

Kentucky's economy must be considered substandard on the basis of almost any national economic indicator. Many farm and mining areas are economically depressed. The average family income in Kentucky in 1959 was $4,051, representing 72 percent of the national figure. In 1959 the average family income in Clay County was under $2,500; that year Clay County was one of sixteen Kentucky counties in which 70 percent or more of the families reported such low incomes.

In 1960 there were some 142,000 recipients of public-assistance programs of various categories in Kentucky. Federal grants in the state amounted to $14.18 per capita, compared with $11.34 for the nation. In Clay County in 1960, as in other low-income counties of Eastern Kentucky, payments in federally subsidized programs per capita were over $40. About 10 percent of the men in Clay County's rural nonfarm population were unemployed in 1960. Despite the great decline in agricultural and mining employment, the proportion of Kentucky workers employed in agriculture (14.3 percent) was still more than twice the national rate (6.7 percent), and those employed in mining industries in the state amounted to four times the national proportion. Less than 10 percent of all employed persons were in manufacturing industries in Clay County in 1960; 20 to 25 percent of all employed persons were in white-collar occupations (professional, managerial, clerical, and sales).

In Clay County as in other counties of Eastern Kentucky, the educational level of heads of households is typically low. In Clay County in 1960 the average number of years of schooling completed by persons twenty-five years of age and older was under 7.5 (the national average was 10.6 years); Clay County shared this rate with nine other Kentucky counties. Under 70 percent of the Clay County children sixteen and seventeen years of age were enrolled in school in 1960 (the national average was 80.9). In 1964, 75 percent of Clay County's 5,800 school-age children were in schools having 100 or more pupils. There is a consolidated high school (grades 9-12) in the county, and ten regional, consolidated elementary schools. In addition, there are thirty-five one-teacher schools, five two-teacher schools, and three three-teacher schools (grades 1-8).

Lying partly in the Eastern coalfields and partly in the Eastern Kentucky hills area, Clay County has been economically dependent on mining, small-scale agriculture, and lumbering. As small, marginal farms became unprofitable, and coal miners were displaced as a consequence of restricted mining production and, increasingly, of the introduction of more efficient mining equipment, a surplus male labor force was created. Many out-migrated either alone or with their families to seek employment in the industrialized north-central states. Many remained behind to increase the high rate of the unemployed in Kentucky. Much of the failure of these displaced workers to become employed in other occupations stems from their lack of basic education, which acts as a barrier to their being trained in other technical skills. In addition, new industries have not materialized in Eastern Kentucky in sufficient quantity to absorb the displaced workers and young people entering the labor force. Moreover, many of these men have little or no experience living outside the mountains and often have no desire to leave their home. Jack Weller aptly describes the psychological effect of these combined factors as "the shock of unemployability."

Not all residents of Southern Appalachia, however, are adversely affected by the economic problems of the region. James Brown, another rural sociologist at the University of Kentucky, has observed: "Casual observers and, too often, trained social scientists as well, tend to view the populations of rural low-income areas as relatively homogeneous 'pockets of poverty.' Too often they fail to take into account that systems of social stratification exist within such depressed areas or, to phrase it another way, that families in such areas vary in their abilities to cope with the problems of survival and of assuring the well-being of family members in a situation of continual economic crisis."[3]

THE LIFE-STYLE

Much of the writing on the life-style of the Southern Appalachian highlander by sociologists and anthropologists at the end of the last century, and more recently in our own time, has, in summary, consisted largely of a careful cataloging of his methods of adapting to his circumstances. These writers generally see the mountaineer's attitudes as having developed primarily during the last century, but being maintained largely unchanged to the present day. Many of these writers have contributed much of value in describing the attitudes, values, mores, and adjustive or coping methods people characteristically used in the southern mountains.[4] Much of this writing has focused on the life-style of the very poor or of the region's working class. However, most of the writers assert that a substantial legacy of values, standards, attitudes, and adaptive methods has come down to Appalachian people of all three socioeconomic classes from their common mountaineer background. Like legacies anywhere, it is a legacy of both strengths and weaknesses, of attitudes adequate to direct the daily lives of people who habitually use them and attitudes that are inadequate for the tasks at hand.

Jack Weller, in his book *Yesterday's People,* compares the frontier attitudes of the original mountaineer with the ones that were gradually formed by his descendants. Weller, a Presbyterian minister, has spent many years living and working among people of the Southern Appalachian region. As an outsider he had gained objective insights into many aspects of the minds and lives of southern highlanders and has recorded his impressions with both clarity and compassion.

Weller and the other writers cited focus initially on the fierce independence of the early settlers in the southern mountains. It was an absolutely essential trait for survival. The geographic isolation of families in the hills reinforced the pattern of each individual's depending upon his own talent, strength, and resourcefulness. Thus, cooperative social activities were rare in mountain life; families made their own way. Isolation, interacting with independence, in time worked a change in the old self-reliance of the highlander. His independence became individualism, a more self-centered trait. All that he does has himself in focus. Group activities are engaged in only to the extent that his private ends are served. Weller concludes: "This independence-turned-individualism, a corruption of the virtue which was once the foundation stone of the mountain man's way of life, now proves to be a great stumbling block to his finding a place in our increasingly complex and cooperative society."[5]

A second significant trait of the mountaineer is traditionalism. He is bound to the past, its traditions, ideas, and values. Through the years his outlook has been regressive, to the old ways. These ways maintained the mountaineer in an existence-oriented society, whose goals lay in meeting only the very basic survival needs. Unlike the contemporary American middle-class person, the tradition-oriented highlander is not improvement oriented, nor does he confidently anticipate the future as a motivating force in his life. Weller concludes:

[Today's]mountain youth are the least traditionalistic; yet the tendency is still prevalent, even in them. They are not ready and eager for new ideas and new experiences, but cling closely to the forms and clichés that are the bulwarks of the older generation. This existence orientation makes the whole society very conservative in every aspect of its life, almost passive in accepting the status quo, for things are all right as they are and change seems always for the worse. Even for the youth, the tomorrows are looked upon not with a sense of challenge and adventure but with suspicion and some trepidation.[6]

Within the mountain subculture a third trait, fatalism, was gradually developed as a way of coping with the chronic sense of failure experienced by highlanders as their land limited and defeated them. Fatalism enabled the mountaineer to feel his life was fundamentally right even when he was discouraged by it. The trait nowhere found clearer expression than in mountain religion. All Protestant denominations and sects in the region accept hard lives and times as "God's will—He wants it this way. Who am I to complain?"

A fourth characteristic of the mountaineer was his action-orientation. He, like the natural rhythms of life about him in the hills, was episodic and impulsive. These traits, again, were opposed to the routine-seeking orientation of the American middle class. The mountaineer avoided routine-oriented events and institutions as boring, not satisfying. He disliked steady, time-oriented jobs, regular schooling, routine committee meetings, routine churchgoing, and other activities calling for a methodical application of time and personal effort.

Another characteristic of the mountaineer was his stoicism. In adapting to the daily apprehensions of his rigorous life with its many stresses, the mountaineer turned inward, covering his intense anxieties with denial and silence. His underlying fearfulness, Weller feels, finds open expression in one characteristic child-rearing practice: children are often made to obey through fear. "Something will happen to you—you'll get hit on the road by the truck, or someone will take you away from here—if you don't mind." This particular child-rearing practice revealed the mountaineer's long-standing realistic concern that the outside environment was, indeed, often harsh, cruel, and fear-provoking.

A final characteristic of the mountaineer underscored by Weller, the conceptualization of which he attributes to Herbert Gans,[7] was his person-orientation. The highlander personalized his thoughts, words, actions, and relationships. He was not oriented to objects—outside goals, principles, things, jobs—but to people. His concern was to be a person within his group. His constant desire to be noticed, accepted, and liked by other members of his group was a life goal in itself. It accounted for the mountaineer's deep sensitivity to real or implied criticism of himself by others. On the other hand, the trait underscored the deep abiding person-to-person relationships the mountaineer, in time, often makes with others. He is much more oriented to keeping his friendly relationships with others than with doing business or keeping to a schedule. As Weller puts it:

In the [Southern Appalachian] folk culture, you don't just step in for a moment to check on a detail or two of business, then move on. Each contact is a person-to-person encounter, and this takes time— hours of it. A trip to the store, going to the neighbors to borrow a cup of sugar or an ax, meeting a friend on the road—these are not impersonal encounters, in which the business at hand can be done quickly, but are the occasions for the kinds of personal relationships that form the very core of the mountain man's existence.[8]

The Southern Appalachian highlander in the transitional period of history between the frontier and today was required, inevitably perhaps, to develop the personality traits of individualism, traditionalism, religious fatalism, an action-orientation, stoicism in manner and speech, and an intense person-orientation. These traits enabled him to adapt to the stresses of a time that followed the passing of the frontier. However, the same traits, passed on essentially unchanged to many present-day Appalachian people, make it exceedingly difficult for the person possessing these traits to adapt to the relatively impersonal, goal-oriented, routine-seeking ways of most contemporary Americans. Evidence of the clash of these two quite different life-styles is abundant today in two general arenas. They clash as middle-class professionals from outside the mountain culture move into the Southern Appalachian region in attempts to assist in effecting change and betterment in the people and their ways, and as hordes of Appalachian migrants move into urban centers and for the first time mix with others of quite different background. Each group has often found it difficult to understand the other. Finding it difficult, each group frequently withdraws to itself. Middle-class Americans often reject the Appalachian dweller or migrant as "too stupid," "too lazy," or "too different." I found this point of particular relevance when I was formulating the factors in redirecting regional child development that are discussed in Part II.

In writing about regional educational needs in *The Southern Appalachian Region: A Survey,* Orin Graff indicates from his review of the data based on a sample of the region's schools in the early 1960s that "the Southern Appalachian region has made considerable progress in education since 1935. On the other hand, its progress has been so little when compared with that of the states or the nation as a whole as to merely dramatize its loss of pace."[9]

For example, in 1950 Southern Appalachian residents twenty-five years of age and older were significantly less well educated than the same age group in the nation as a whole; the median school years completed by persons twenty-five and older was 9.3 for the nation and 7.2 for the region. The regional median at that time was less than the median for any state in the union and less than that for any other economic region in the nation.[10] By 1958 the regional median for completed years of schooling for heads of households had risen appreciably, to 9.3; however, there still did not appear to be any narrowing of the gap between the regional and national educational levels. Through all these figures ran the observation that the lowest levels of education were, and remain, associated with the lower socioeconomic class in the Southern Appalachian region.

Graff and others have felt that the lower educational level of many Southern Appalachian communities, particularly among lower-class family members, is related to the lack of holding power of the schools. This lack of holding power is a condition of serious proportions, creating a heavy burden in view of the correlation between low income and low education. For example, a sample study revealed that high school seniors in the Southern Appalachian rural school systems in 1947 represented about one-fourth of those who were in the sixth grade in 1941; only one-half of the same 1941 sixth graders were in the ninth grade in 1944.[11] The metropolitan systems in the region did somewhat better in holding their students. Between 1953 and 1959 further data indicated that even though improvement in the holding power of regional schools was marked, these same sample systems were still losing pupils at the rate of 10 to 20 percent between the sixth and ninth grades and from 44 to 63 percent before high school graduation.

Eastern Kentucky shared in these regional trends. In 1961 the Kentucky State Department of Education released figures showing steadily increasing holding power for Kentucky high schools following substantial annual increases in state aid to local schools beginning in 1956. For example, 55.5 percent of all ninth-grade Kentucky students completed public high school in 1956; this percentage rose to 61.4 by 1960. The comparable national average for 1960 was about 60 percent. These figures, however, do not show the specific drop-out rates for Eastern Kentucky students, which have been appreciably higher, particularly for the lower class, than these figures for the state as a whole.

Eastern Kentucky schools in the past have had problems both in administration and in financing. Local boards of education, which decide upon school administrative matters, often lack a share in deciding local fiscal matters that affect the educational program. These boards generally have no power to set a school-tax levy within prescribed limits or even to call for referenda on budget proposals. In addition, the quality of key school administrators varies widely in the region. Some superintendents of schools, for example, are professionally trained and dedicated school executives. Other superintendents, however, are county politicians rather than professional school administrators; they may even be political opponents of members of their own boards of education. School programs often become political footballs, caught between opposing community interests. In addition, most communities lack the economic ability to support adequate educational programs.

These local exigencies have been somewhat balanced in recent years, however, by the considerable financial support from federal tax sources. Many new consolidated and vocational training schools have been built with these funds in the past several years. Most school administrators in the area have felt that improvement in the local school programs is virtually impossible without this federal aid to education.

Other factors also affect Eastern Kentucky school programs. Although Kentucky has a statewide compulsory school-attendance law, it is not enforced in several Eastern Kentucky counties. Salaries for elementary and secondary teachers, though currently improving, are still low when compared with those in other states. In recent years far fewer teachers hold positions on emergency certificates; a majority now have completed college education. However, teachers in the region are still almost a year behind the national average in completed years of college preparation. Nevertheless, some Eastern Kentucky counties no longer have a teacher shortage; some, in fact, can choose their teaching staffs from an applicant pool that is larger than the number of available positions.

Despite these past or current deficiencies, the educational programs in Eastern Kentucky are showing steady improvement. A key factor in eventual promotion of even further gains of all types in local school programs will be the changing attitudes of the people themselves, the consumers of the program. Recent surveys have shown that Eastern Kentucky residents favor consolidation of the schools and compulsory school attendance to age sixteen and that many respondents want a better education for their children than they had themselves. Such attitudinal shifts will provide important improvement-oriented support for local boards of education in their planning of future school programs. Furthermore, there is evidence from many quarters in Eastern Kentucky today that education is indeed becoming an effective bridge between the values and standards of contemporary national life and the attitudes and ways of people living in the region.

CHAPTER 13   Operation
of the
Field
Clinics

During the initial six years of operation of the Manchester Project, 287
emotionally troubled children and
their families were referred to our
field mental health clinics for diagnostic evaluation and treatment. An
additional group of 650 children were
discussed in case consultations at local
schools. The majority of clinic referrals were made by the senior public
health nurses from their district case
loads. School personnel and local
physicians also referred families, but
always through the nursing staffs at
the health departments. In this way,
referrals took advantage of the nurses'
intimate knowledge of and proximity
to the community, its families, and its
resources. Through traditional public
health programs and their positions
as school nurses, the public health
nurses played a key role in the early
finding of troubled children. Many
of the 287 referrals in fact were early
ones, and all were appropriate.
    Following the decision for referral
of a particular child and before the
family was seen in the field clinic,

the case was thoroughly reviewed by the nurse in whose district the child lived and attended school. In this initial or diagnostic phase, the nurse's role merged with the traditional role of the psychiatric social worker. The nurse visited the child in his school setting, talked with him in the classroom, watched him at recess, and conferred with his teachers. Current and past medical information was gathered from the child's local physician and from any health-care or social agencies with whom the family may have been involved. The nurse then visited the home. There she talked for several hours with parents, grandparents, aunts, and uncles. She again talked with the child and watched him at work and play in a variety of relationships with adults, his brothers and sisters, and neighborhood children.

The nurse then arranged appointments for the family at the health department and on clinic days presented her findings to the traveling part of the project team. Most of the families readily accepted referral. They viewed the mental health clinic as positively as they regarded the other public health programs, an opinion reinforced by the fact of the initial review's being carried out by the familiar and accepted public health nurse.

Several families were initially reluctant to accept referral. Most of these were poor and lived under chronic exposure of many kinds of impoverishment—economic, physical, emotional, and cultural. Like most poor families under severe and chronic stress, they lived in apathy, without hope, and perceived few alternative solutions to their problems. Hence they remained apathetic toward, openly apprehensive about, or even puzzled by a clinic referral as a potentially helpful aid in problem-solving. It was apparent that these tensions had to be eliminated before the clinic could render regular services to these families. By virtue of her shared cultural background, her proximity to families, and her availability in action-oriented, "visible" public health programs, the nurse became the most effective member of the mental health team in overcoming these tensions. Time-consuming though they were, frequent home contacts by the nurses were generally effective in breaking through the barriers of apathy and resistance and in rendering these families more receptive to the clinic phase of needed mental health services.

Several families, because of the nature of the shared family psychopathology (as in several cases of school-phobic reaction), remained fearful of the referral. They expressed their fears by missing initial clinic appointments. If this occurred, the nurse, the social worker, and the psychiatrist promptly visited the family in their home. Often this was successful in overcoming initial resistance and moving the family toward the health department for succeeding appointments. At the health department, parents were interviewed together by the social worker while the child was being seen by the psychiatrist.

Collaboration between all members of the project team followed this initial interview. The findings of all team members were discussed, leading toward an initial dynamic understanding of the child's and the family's problems. Decisions were made for interim, short-term, and long-term treatment. The nurses carried out many of these initial and final case recommendations. They were responsible for prompt follow-up reports to the local family physicians and for follow-up reports and future consultations to the child's school.

In many instances, nurses worked with children and their parents directly under our psychiatric supervision. Some of the families returned to the health departments for short-term, crisis-oriented, or long-term, intensive casework and psychotherapy services provided by the other members of the team.

THE SCHOOL CONSULTATION PROGRAM

All the nurses have, from the very beginning of our joint work, discussed with school administrators the need for a program of case consultation with local teachers. This program, now a regular feature of each field-clinic day, remains a paradigm of the ways in which the nurses have promoted, and continued to support, local mental health services for children.

The project's psychiatrists and social workers, accompanied by the public health nurses in their role of district school nurses in the county, regularly provided these case consultations to schools and to Head Start and day-care programs. A pattern was established whereby each consultation team worked for several months at one particular school, then moved on to another. This allowed us to establish a real working relationship with the teachers. This pattern held true, on the whole, for all four counties served by the Manchester Project. Approximately 650 maladjusting preschool and school-age children were discussed with teachers during the initial six years of the project's operation.

The nurses' participation in the consultation program was crucial for the success of each of its several phases. The initial phase was for the consultant to develop understanding of the teacher's background, her classroom functions, and the way she had come to feel about the particular child being discussed. We found, as T. P. Millar discovered in his work,[1] that our first concern as consultants had to be the teacher's feelings, for until these had been dealt with she was not in a position to accept a different view of the child—the dynamic view accounting for his particular behavior. In this situation, as in her clinic work with families, the cultural background that the nurse shared with the teacher often enabled her to empathize quickly. This made it possible for the consultant to encourage the teacher to express her frustrations more directly; the teacher simply followed the example of the nurse, who was saying clearly how she had felt in a somewhat similar situation. The nurse then joined the consultant in accepting the teacher's direct expression of her feelings, thereby dissipating some of their intensity. After this had happened, and the teacher had been assured of the competence and interest of the consultant (this assurance itself was fostered by the nurse's working relationship with the consultant), she was ready to understand the child in different terms.

The second phase, in which everyone mutually came to understand the child's behavior, received a powerful impetus from the nurse's knowledge of his home background and its psychological, economic, and cultural forces. The teacher and the nurse shared their respective data, often being able to come to a clear conclusion.

The consultant team was then in a position to make classroom management proposals that would help the teacher deal more effectively with the child in the classroom. Sometimes these proposals involved a role for the nurse as well, that of working directly with the child's family. She on occasion neutralized chronic parental concerns about separation, illness, death, and violence, which together had fostered chronic anxiety that was expressed by the children in classroom belligerence, to cite one example.

Occasionally it was necessary for the nurse to follow up the regular consultation by visits with the teacher in her classroom. This was done when the teacher's changed attitudes toward a child began to fade. The nurse's continuing supportive consultation tended to reinforce the teacher's desirable attitude change, and this was accompanied by more effective classroom management of the child.

CHAPTER 14   Mental
                Health
                of the
                Very Poor

The term *very poor*, as used here and
as used by others,[1] refers to those
families in Eastern Kentucky who live
at the bottom of the socioeconomic
ladder, as distinguished from those
poor who are one rung up this ladder
—the generally self-sufficient and at
least moderately successful working-
class families. The very poor include
individuals who have extremely limited employment skills. They are
usually unskilled, casual laborers who
remain chronically unemployed or
severely underemployed. They are
apt to have less than a fourth-grade
education; many are illiterate or only
barely able to read and write. For
the most part, they come from families
in which lack of education, lack of
steady employment, and lack of adequate income have tended to be the
rule for several generations. These
families in Eastern Kentucky, as elsewhere in the nation, are often referred to as the "hard-core poor"—
and this hard core seems to be the
axis of the "cycle of poverty."[2] The
situations underlying the terms *cycle*

of poverty (poverty that extends from generation to generation) and the *culture of poverty* (the distinguishing folkways of the very poor) have been the subject of regional writing for years. Novelists, poets, minstrels, sociologists, government researchers, politicians, and industrialists have described the lives of the very poor, not only in Eastern Kentucky but in the wider Southern Appalachian region.

These writers have told but one aspect of the Appalachian story—the feuds, the inadequate agriculture, the harsh life of the mining towns, the terrible mining accidents, the shocking illiteracy rate, the poverty, the squalor, and the chronically high incidence of disease. Harry Caudill describes the Southern Appalachian very poor as "the product of initial backwoods intransigence followed by generations of isolation, poor schools, and governmental neglect."[3]

Some of the stories have been highly romanticized and over-idealized, as though the very poor in the Southern Appalachian region were a happy lot of folk. In contrast however, Thomas Ford says about the lives of this group:

[There are] two general attributes of families in poverty as they relate specifically to Appalachian families. The first of these attributes is the severe stress under which such families must operate as a result of their chronic exposure to a great number and variety of severe problems. The second is the limited number of alternative solutions to these problems which they perceive as being available to them.

There is much evidence to support the proposition that poor families live under great stress. They typically have high rates of disease, disability, and mortality. They are also afflicted by poor housing, inadequate education, family problems, and, of course, economic problems of various kinds. Despite this, there is still a great deal of romantic nonsense abroad in the land that the poor—especially those who reside in rural Appalachia—live relatively carefree existences. Some of the information the Department of Sociology at the University of Kentucky has recently reported in a publication entitled *Mountain Families in Poverty*[4] should help dispel this fantasy, although myths of this nature have a remarkable vitality. Let it suffice to say that the problems faced by most of these [very poor] Eastern Kentucky families in their daily existence makes the most crisis-laden television soap opera seem bland fare in comparison. It might be added that the data in the cited study do not support another myth about the poor, namely, that they are not greatly concerned about the adverse conditions under which they live. On the contrary, there is considerable evidence that the mental and emotional strain upon the family members is quite severe, even though it may not be apparent to the casual observer.[5]

The mental health implications of this severe and chronic stress suffered by very poor families in Eastern Kentucky have been traced out earlier in this book. Certainly the very poor in the region do seem to have more than their share of mental retardation and mental disorder. Taking the matter of protracted stress broadly, however, one can examine the characteristic ways by which very poor families attempt to cope with such stress. How do they try to handle their problems? What techniques available to them seem adaptive, and which do not? We have much empirical evidence to suggest that in the past, on the whole, the very poor in the region have coped with stress only partially or have not been able to cope well at all. In fact, their failures to cope leave the anxieties and strains raised by stress largely raw, unbound.

The relatively rigid, fatalistic, nonverbal, anti-intellectual lifestyle of the very poor is closely associated with unbound, raw anxiety. Lacking, on the whole, adequate ways of relieving anxiety, the very poor in the region characteristically bow down under the sheer weight of it. They develop an apathetic, resigned, careworn appearance; helpless-hopeless inner feelings; and silent personal withdrawal from tasks and from other people. Such a state, called "the poverty syndrome" by many, can be conceptualized as a chronic psychological depression. Others in addition to our clinical team have taken note that, lacking other defenses against their anxieties and this depression, a number of the very poor find temporary escape in such expressive activities as fantasy, dramatic behavior, psychophysiologic and conversion reactions, impulsive acts, and alcohol. Quite often, we have found, the behavior and emotional disorders of the very poor can be interpreted overall as depressed surrender to failure that is perceived by them as inevitable. Like an animal caught in a trap, the very poor tend at times to lie still, in quiet, withdrawn, conservation-of-energies patterns; at other times, they, like the trapped, kick out in desperate, futile attempts to escape.

Ford examines further the adjustive techniques and failures to cope with severe and protracted stress characteristic of the very poor in Appalachia:

There are a number of reasons why poor families do not perceive many alternative solutions to their problems. The most obvious, of course, is that remedial services cost money, which low-income families do not have. But lack of money is not the only restrictive factor. Being less informed in general, the poor are less likely to know where to turn for help, even when it is without cost to them. In the case of most isolated areas of Appalachia, there has actually not been very much assistance of the kinds we might find readily available in urban areas. Community institutions have been, and still are, relatively underdeveloped. Consequently, the family has been virtually the only institution upon which they could depend.

Dr. Looff has been concerned with the psychopathology evidenced by many of these families, especially by the children. Whether there is a greater prevalence of psychopathology among Appalachian families has not been established, because needed epidemiological studies have not been carried out. There are logical grounds for expecting this to be the case, however. In the first place, there is a greater amount of poverty and its attendant problems and strains. In the second place, the family itself has been virtually the only major social mechanism available to absorb these strains. In many respects the extended family network has done a remarkable job of handling the burdens of poverty, in part by spreading the problems over a larger number of persons who are obligated to assist their kinfolk in times of severe need. With extensive out-migration, as has occurred in recent decades, it has become increasingly difficult for the extended family to function in its traditional manner. Undoubtedly this has served to increase the stress on many families in the region, and probably at a faster rate than community institutions have been able to provide relief.[6]

THE NATIONAL PICTURE

There are dangers in generalizing from the traits of one particular poverty group to all others. Nonetheless, there are points of data on which the very poor in Eastern Kentucky can be compared with the very poor elsewhere in the nation.

Physicians and other students of medicine are becoming well aware of the influence of geographic location on poverty and of the phenomenon of clustering of physical and social pathologies. Poverty-stricken areas in Eastern Kentucky, like those elsewhere in the nation, are usually marked by disease, substandard housing, inadequate education, broken homes, and chronic unemployment. Poverty and disease are often inseparable: abundant statistical data indicate that the poor have higher death rates for tuberculosis, cancer of the cervix, cardiovascular-renal disease, influenza, pneumonia, and home accidents. They have more mental disorders and mental retardation, more births per 100,000 inhabitants, more illegitimate births, more pregnancies with little or no prenatal care, an infant mortality rate two or three times as high as that in more affluent sections, more orthopedic and visual impairments, and a host of other often preventable and correctable conditions.

A notable speech summarizing the general health problems

of the poor concluded thus: "However meaningful these general statistics may be, they cannot reveal the suffering, despair and apathy that we know exist in unmeasured quantity among the poor."[7]

In stating her national perspective of the mental health problems of the poor, Viola Bernard spoke for the growing number of social and community psychiatrists when she said: "We know that there are many kinds of impoverishment—economic, physical, emotional, cultural, and intellectual. Despite some promising investigations of causal relationships between environmental circumstances and mental disorders, there is much in that whole area that is as yet unclear. We do have evidence, however, that poverty in combination with social disorganization is frequently psychopathogenic, in contrast to poverty when various other social conditions prevail. *Accordingly, the psychosocial and psychopathological correlates of poverty rest on a tremendous number of variables,* so that the psychiatric treatment of choice for patients who are poor must correspondingly vary."[8]

This theme of the variability of the psychopathological correlates of poverty has been illustrated by several programs for the poor from around the nation.

In a carefully conceived and conducted family program in Boston, Eleanor Pavenstedt compared two groups of lower-class urban families as child-rearing environments. Her description of the difference in maturation and behavior of the children in these two groups of families—a so-called stable working-class (or upper-lower-class) group, and a socially disorganized (or lower-lower-class) group—convincingly demonstrates the error of oversimplified psychiatric generalizations about the "underprivileged, or poor," as if they were a single category.[9]

Similarly, the psychological strengths and the degree of emotional health reported by Robert Coles from his observations of impoverished southern Negro children living under conditions of severe environmental stress are in sharp contrast to the kinds of serious psychopathology observed by Edgar Auerswald and his co-workers in children at the Wiltwyck School for Boys, a treatment facility in New York. These intensely deprived New York slum children, from socially disorganized and psychologically impoverished as well as economically impoverished families, could seldom be helped by traditional psychotherapeutic approaches.[10]

These types of mental illness are yet again different from

the emotional problems of the migrant poor. In a study of migrant farm laborers, Robert Coles reports: "The constant movement, the threat of social chaos, the cramped living and traveling, make for common problems and remarkably similar responses to them which separate to some extent migrant behavior from that of the rest of the poor. Indeed, we are in general perhaps ill-advised to lump millions of poor people together—at least psychologically—on the basis of their common relative lack of income."[11]

Thus, the more we know of the external forces involved in mental illness, the more we understand the complex connection between individual and social pathology. In the preface of their book *Mental Health of the Poor*, the editors conclude: "The effects of social class on mental health are uneven and complex. We are suspect of viewpoints espousing one-to-one relationships between class position and mental illness. *Analysis of the poor is best directed through appraisal of various subgroupings rather than the disadvantaged as a whole, or any common denominator thereof.*"[12]

This point is certainly confirmed by the personality and attitudes of the Appalachian lower class. Their hard lives give rise to personal attitudes of fierce individualism, traditionalism, and fatalism. On the other hand, unlike many of the very poor elsewhere in the nation, the very poor in Eastern Kentucky retain basic relatedness, a capacity for basic trustfulness in relationships with others. In this respect, the basically sound capacity for relating with others possessed by the very poor in Eastern Kentucky is like the object-relationship capacities displayed by the stable working-class families studied in several urban settings. Another way of stating this is to indicate that the very poor in Eastern Kentucky are not essentially socially disorganized; in this respect, they are unlike the lower-lower-class, or very poor, families studied in Boston by Eleanor Pavenstedt. However, the very poor in Eastern Kentucky do share not only the hard lot of the very poor elsewhere in the nation, but another characteristic as well: the interacting, reinforcing factors of physical, mental, and cultural isolation operate to hold them in disadvantaged areas, frequently resisting changes that would bring them into effective contact with the outside world.

In this book I have discussed ways of approaching those who put up this resistance, ways of answering their calls for help—

calls that often must be painstakingly deciphered in the home and in the clinic before they can become the basis for positive, joint action. The rewards are profound. When progress begins, and we are relating to and working with a mountain man in this kind of joint endeavor, we see him beginning that extraordinary experience which all people imbued with new hope undergo—the flowering of their inherent capacity to grow and develop. The people of Eastern Kentucky, and of the Southern Appalachian region, have a remarkably unique history. They have suffered long periods of struggle and despair. They have known economic and personal defeat. But, looking at the other side of the developmental coin, one can see that these people possess also certain unique qualities. Many from the region have already utilized these strengths to build their own lives. Others, less fortunate, have yet to do so. But the strengths are there for them as well—latent, yet to be fully tapped—but present nonetheless.

Notes

CHAPTER 1

1. George R. Stewart, *Names on the Land* (New York, 1945).

CHAPTER 2

1. The interviews were initially open-ended, followed by structured, task-oriented questions. Verbatim notes of the interviews were analyzed; the information was written into a research schedule that was divided by age and subdivided by developmental tasks under the various psychosocial stages of development. Detailed observations of parent–child interactions were recorded in similar manner. The research schedule was adapted for my use in Eastern Kentucky from one devised by Janet Newman, M.D., a child psychiatrist at the University of Cincinnati College of Medicine. I am indebted to Dr. Newman for her permission to use the schedule in my work.

2. Jack E. Weller, *Yesterday's People: Life in Contemporary Appalachia* (Lexington, Ky., 1965), pp. 61-62.

CHAPTER 3

1. The patient was seen in psychiatric consultation by Abraham Wikler, M.D. (professor of psychiatry in the Department of Psychiatry, University of Kentucky Medical Center), to whom I am indebted for sharing with me data pertinent to the case.

2. Louise B. Gerrard, "The Rural Folk of Southern West Virginia," West Virginia Department of Mental Health (March 1966), pp. 7-9.

3. Ibid., pp. 9-11.

CHAPTER 4

1. Jack Weller also emphasizes this point. See *Yesterday's People: Life in Contemporary Appalachia* (Lexington, Ky., 1965), pp. 49, 62.

2. Leon Eisenberg, "School Phobia," in *Pediatric Clinics of North America* (Philadelphia, 1958), pp. 645-66; Melitta Sperling, "School Phobias—Classification, Dynamics, and Treatment," in *Psychoanalytic Study of the Child* (New York, 1967), 22:375-401; S. Waldfogel, J. Coolidge, and P. Hahn, "The Development, Meaning, and Management of School Phobia," *American Journal of Orthopsychiatry* 27 (1957): 754-62.

3. Samuel Waldfogel and George Gardner, "Intervention in Crisis as a Method of Primary Prevention," in *Prevention of Mental Disorders in Children*, ed. Gerald Caplan (New York, 1961).

4. David H. Looff and Mary N. Smith, "School Phobia in the Southern Appalachian Region: Crucial Importance of Early Treatment," *Southern Medical Journal* 62, no. 3 (March 1969): 329-35.

5. The diagnostic category of overly dependent personality disorder is discussed in Group for the Advancement of Psychiatry, *Psychopathological Disorders in Childhood: Theoretical Considerations and a Proposed Classification*, Report no. 62 (June 1966): 241-42; hereafter cited as *Group for the Advancement of Psychiatry Report No. 62*.

6. The diagnostic category of deviations in social development is discussed in ibid., pp. 225-28.

7. It has been recommended that the term symbiotic psychosis, used operationally by many child psychiatry centers for years, be replaced by the term interactional psychosis. The diagnostic category is discussed in *Group for the Advancement of Psychiatry Report No. 62*, pp. 253-54. See also an early report by Margaret Mahler, "On Childhood Psychosis and Schizophrenia: Autistic and Symbiotic Infantile Psychosis," in *Psychoanalytic Study of the Child* (New York, 1952), 7: 286-305.

8. The crude data here are from the adult outpatient clinics and wards of the University of Kentucky Medical Center. Prominent among the psychophysiologic disorders of adult patients from Eastern Kentucky are psychogenic headache, peptic ulcer, and low-back pain, which affect both men and women. In addition, in women, various menstrual irregularities often have a major psychological component.

9. A discussion of psychophysiologic disorders is contained in *Group for the Advancement of Psychiatry Report No. 62*, pp. 258-62. See also Hale F. Shirley, *Pediatric Psychiatry* (Cambridge, Mass., 1963), pp. 538-79.

10. W. W. Schottstaedt, *Psychophysiologic Approach in Medical Practice* (Chicago, 1960).

11. E. Miller, "Psychiatric Aspects of Psychosomatic Research," in *Psychosomatic Aspects of Pediatrics*, ed. R. MacKeith and J. Sandler (New York, 1961), p. 139.

12. New York, 1960.

13. Thomas Szasz, *The Myth of Mental Illness* (New York, 1961), pp. 108-9.

14. Edwin A. Weinstein, personal communication, 1967. See also Edwin A. Weinstein, "Cultural Factors in Conversion Hysteria," in *Culture Change, Mental Health, and Poverty*, ed. Joseph C. Finney (Lexington, Ky., 1969).

15. The term early infantile autism was introduced into child psychiatry in this country by Leo Kanner. See Leo Kanner, "Problems of Nosology and Psychodynamics of Early Infantile Autism," *American Journal of Orthopsychiatry* 10 (1949): 416-26. The term primary behavior disorder is used by many child psychiatrists of different training and theoretical backgrounds.

16. Erik H. Erikson, *Childhood and Society*, 2d ed. (New York, 1963).

17. Early infantile autism is discussed in *Group for the Advancement of Psychiatry Report No. 62*, p. 253.

18. Primary behavior disorders are discussed in ibid., pp. 245-48. In this report they are termed an impulse-ridden personality disorder.

19. See Eleanor Pavenstedt, "A Comparison of a Child-Rearing Environment of Upper-Lower and Very Low-Lower Class Families," *American Journal of Orthopsychiatry* 35 (1965): 89-98.

20. Erik H. Erikson, "Growth and Crisis of the Healthy Personality," in *Problems of Infancy and Childhood*, ed. Milton J. E. Senn (New York, 1950), Supplement 2.

21. See Weller, *Yesterday's People;* also helpful toward the concept of a "personalization of services" in a therapeutic sense in our work with Eastern Kentucky families was Marion Pearsall's *Little Smokey Ridge* (Tuscaloosa, Ala., 1959).

CHAPTER 5

1. James T. Proctor, "Hysteria in Childhood," *American Journal of Orthopsychiatry* 28 (1958): 394-407. Proctor found conversion reactions occurring in both Negro and white children of all ages, with equal frequency in boys and girls.

2. Weston LaBarre, *They Shall Take Up Serpents: The Southern Snake Cult* (Durham, N. C., 1956).

3. Conversion reactions are discussed in *Group for the Advancement of Psychiatry Report No. 62*, under psychoneurotic disorder, conversion type, pp. 233-34. For further current definition see also Hale F. Shirley, *Pediatric Psychiatry* (Cambridge, Mass., 1963), pp. 591-93.

4. Wilfred Abse, "Hysteria," in *American Handbook of Psychiatry*, ed. Silvana Arieti (New York, 1959), p. 274.

5. David H. Looff, "Psychophysiologic and Conversion Reactions in Children: Selective Incidence in Verbal and Nonverbal Families," *Journal of the American Academy of Child Psychiatry*, 9, no. 2 (April 1970): 318-31.

6. Hysterical personality disorders are discussed in *Group for the Advancement of Psychiatry Report No. 62*, pp. 240-41.

7. Margaret Mitchell, *Gone with the Wind* (New York, 1936).

8. C. H. Thigpen and H. M. Cleckley, *The Three Faces of Eve* (New York, 1957).

9. Anxious personality disorders are discussed in *Group for the Advancement of Psychiatry Report No. 62*, p. 241.

10. Oppositional personality disorders are discussed in ibid., p. 242.

CHAPTER 6

1. Overly inhibited personality disorders are discussed in *Group for the Advancement of Psychiatry Report No. 62*, pp. 242-43.
2. Fred R. Eggan, personal communication, 1966.
3. This point is frequently made by those attending the annual Workshop on the Urban Adjustment of Southern Appalachian Migrants held at Berea College in Kentucky. These workshops, sponsored by the Council of the Southern Mountains, Inc., seek to promote a more widespread urban understanding of the situation from which Southern Appalachian migrants come and to sensitize urban leaders to the customs, cultural values, and attitudes with which migrants arrive.
4. M. Tramer, "Elektiver Mutismus bei Kindern," *Zeitschrift für Kinderpsychiatrie* 1 (1934): 30-35.
5. E. Pustrom and R. W. Speers, "Elective Mutism in Children," *Journal of the American Academy of Child Psychiatry* 3, no. 2 (1964): 287-97.
6. Weller, *Yesterday's People: Life in Contemporary Appalachia* (Lexington, Ky., 1965), pp. 40-43.

CHAPTER 7

1. Catherine Chilman, *Growing Up Poor*, U.S., Department of Health, Education, and Welfare, Welfare Administration Publication no. 13 (May 1966), p. 32.
2. Subsequently, an OEO-funded community action program was begun in this county. One of its features is a day-care program for children of the very poor in part of the region. Homemaker demonstration services are provided for the mothers of the children in the nursery school. The nurse-consultant for the program is the one who guided the work with Danny's family.

CHAPTER 8

1. *Group for the Advancement of Psychiatry Report No. 62*. This classification was chosen for our field clinic work and for this book because 1) the proposed classification represents the most recent national consensus of child psychiatrists and others regarding nomenclature in children's psychopathology; 2) we have found the classification to be operationally useful in our clinical work; and 3) we wished to present our clinical case material by this proposed national classification standard to further communication with those readers who are clinicians.
2. These data comparisons are drawn out in David H. Looff, Mildred B. Gabbard, and Dorothy A. Miller, "The Manchester Project: A Child Psychiatry Clinic in a County Health Department" (Paper delivered at the meeting of the Southeastern Division of the American

Psychiatric Association, Hollywood, Fla., Oct. 24, 1966); David H. Looff, "Appalachian Public Health Nursing: Mental Health Component in Eastern Kentucky," *Community Mental Health Journal* 5, no. 4 (1969): 295-303; David H. Looff, "Psychophysiologic and Conversion Reactions in Children: Selective Incidence in Verbal and Nonverbal Families," *Journal of the American Academy of Child Psychiatry* 9, no. 2 (1970): 318-31.

3. Howard M. Kern, Jr., "Community Psychiatry Training: A Public Health Approach," in *Concepts in Community Psychiatry*, U.S., Public Health Service Publication no. 1319 (1965).

4. Hyman M. Forstenzer, "Planning and Evaluation of Community Mental Health Programs," in *Concepts in Community Psychiatry*, U.S., Public Health Service Publication no. 1319 (1965).

CHAPTER 9

1. John Dollard and Neal E. Miller, *Personality and Psychotherapy* (New York, 1950).

2. Joseph W. Eaton and Robert J. Weil, for example, feel the data they gained from a mental health study of a Hutterite population fit this theory well; see *Culture and Mental Disorders: A Comparative Study of the Hutterites and Other Populations* (Glencoe, N.Y., 1955), p. 135. Adult patients in the Hutterite group had chiefly those neurotic symptoms which were socially acceptable in their culture. They took their tensions out on themselves by internalizing them as depression or psychophysiologic responses. Phobic and obsessive-compulsive reactions, which would violate strong cultural taboos, were rare. Within their highly structured social system, Hutterite individuals also were sufficiently sheltered and guided to make generalized anxiety reactions rare. See also Johann Brenner, "A Social Psychiatric Investigation of a Small Community in Northern Norway," *Acta Psychiatrica et Neurologica*, Supplementum 62 (1951): 50-51.

3. I am indebted to Donald McVarish, developmental psychologist with the Department of Behavioral Science, University of Kentucky Medical Center, for some of the social learning concepts contained in this section.

4. Edwin A. Weinstein, personal communication, 1967. See also Edwin A. Weinstein, "Cultural Factors in Conversion Hysteria," in *Culture Change, Mental Health, and Poverty*, ed. Joseph C. Finney (Lexington, Ky., 1969).

5. Alfred H. Washburn, "Influences of Early Development upon Later Life," in *Relations of Development and Aging*, ed. James E. Birren (Springfield, Ill., 1964), pp. 29-37.

CHAPTER 10

1. See Thomas Ford, "Discussion," following David Looff, "Psychiatric Perspective on Poverty," in *Poverty: New Interdisciplinary*

Perspectives, ed. Thomas Weaver and Alvin Magid (San Francisco, 1969).

2. Jack Weller, *Yesterday's People: Life in Contemporary Appalachia* (Lexington, Ky., 1965), pp. 49-57.

3. Harry K. Schwarzweller and James S. Brown, "Social Class Origins, Rural-Uban Migration, and Economic Life Chances: A Case Study," *Rural Sociology* 32, no. 1 (March 1967): 5-19. See also Harry K. Schwarzweller and John F. Seggar, "Kinship Involvement: A Factor in the Adjustment of Rural Migrants," *Journal of Marriage and the Family* 29, no. 4 (Nov. 1967): 662-71.

4. Saul I. Harrison and John McDermott, "Social Class and Mental Illness in Children," *Archives of General Psychiatry* 13 (1965): 411-17; Norman Q. Brill and Hugh A. Storrow, "Social Class and Psychiatric Treatment," *Archives of General Psychiatry* 3 (1960): 340-44; Betty Overall and Harriet Aronson, "Expectations of Psychotherapy in Patients of Lower Socioeconomic Class," *American Journal of Orthopsychiatry* 33 (1963): 421-30.

CHAPTER 11

1. Thomas Ford, "Discussion," following David Looff, "Psychiatric Perspective on Poverty," in *Poverty: New Interdisciplinary Perspectives,* ed. Thomas Weaver and Alvin Magid (San Francisco, 1969), emphasis added. See also Cyrus M. Johnson, A. Lee Coleman, and William B. Clifford, *Mountain Families in Poverty,* University of Kentucky, Department of Sociology and Kentucky Agricultural Experiment Station, RS-29 (1967).

CHAPTER 12

1. Rupert B. Vance, "Introduction," in Jack E. Weller, *Yesterday's People: Life in Contemporary Appalachia* (Lexington, Ky., 1965), p. vii.

2. Thomas R. Ford, *Health and Demography in Kentucky* (Lexington, Ky., 1964).

3. James S. Brown, "Social Class Origins, Rural-Urban Migration, and Economic Life Chances: A Case Study," *Rural Sociology* 32, no. 1 (March 1967): 5-19.

4. Many references are available in Thomas R. Ford, "The Passing of Provincialism," in *The Southern Appalachian Region: A Survey,* ed. Thomas R. Ford (Lexington, Ky., 1962), pp. 9-34. See particularly Horace Kephart, *Our Southern Highlanders* (New York, 1913); John C. Campbell, *The Southern Highlander and His Homeland* (New York, 1921); Howard Odum, *Southern Regions of the United States* (Chapel Hill, N.C., 1936); Marion Pearsall, *Little Smokey Ridge* (Tuscaloosa, Ala., 1959).

5. *Yesterday's People,* p. 32.

6. Ibid., p. 36.
7. Ibid., p. 50. See Herbert J. Gans, *The Urban Villagers* (New York, 1962), p. 89.
8. Weller, *Yesterday's People,* p. 55.
9. Orin B. Graff, "The Needs of Education," in *The Southern Appalachian Region: A Survey,* ed. Thomas R. Ford (Lexington, Ky., 1962), pp. 188-200.
10. James S. Brown, *Basic Population Data for the Southern Appalachians,* University of Kentucky Social Research Service (Aug. 1958), p. 45.
11. Robert C. DeLozier, "Public School Enrollment Prediction for the Southern Appalachian Region" (M.S. thesis, University of Tennessee, 1959).

CHAPTER 13

1. T. P. Millar, "Psychiatric Consultation with Teachers," *Journal of the American Academy of Child Psychiatry* 5, no. 1 (Jan. 1966): 134-44.

CHAPTER 14

1. Catherine S. Chilman, *Growing Up Poor,* U.S., Department of Health, Education, and Welfare, Welfare Administration Publication no. 13 (May 1966), p. 1.
2. Wilbur Cohen and Eugenia Sullivan, "Poverty in the United States," in *Indicators,* U.S., Department of Health, Education, and Welfare (Feb. 1964), p. 7.
3. Harry M. Caudill, "Foreword," in Jack E. Weller, *Yesterday's People: Life in Contemporary Appalachia* (Lexington, Ky., 1965), p. xiv.
4. Cyrus M. Johnson, A. Lee Coleman, and William B. Clifford, *Mountain Families in Poverty,* University of Kentucky, Department of Sociology Bulletin no. 29 (May 1967).
5. Thomas R. Ford, "Discussion," following David H. Looff, "Psychiatric Perspective on Poverty," in *Poverty: New Interdisciplinary Perspectives,* ed. Thomas Weaver and Alvin Magid (San Francisco, 1969).
6. See ibid.
7. Philip R. Lee, "Creative Federalism and Health Programs for the Poor," *Pharos* (Jan. 1967): 2-6.
8. Viola W. Bernard, "Some Principles of Dynamic Psychiatry in Relation to Poverty," *American Journal of Psychiatry* 122 (1965): 254-66; emphasis added.
9. Eleanor Pavenstedt, "A Comparison of a Child-Rearing Environment of Upper-Lower and Very Low-Lower Class Families," *American Journal of Orthopsychiatry* 35 (1965): 89-98. Pavenstedt and her

co-workers found that the parents in the stable working-class group actively participated with their children in the evolution of basic relationships to each other as differentiated, trusted, cherished individuals. These parents and their children were capable of evoking satisfying action from each other in times of need and displaying mutually responsive communication and affective exchange. The children developed autonomously with the appropriate mastery of skills in the toddler period and basically sound foundations of sex-role differentiation in the later preschool period. Closely related to this emotional-personality development were age-appropriate language and intellectual-cognitive skills, with the exception of some cultural-stimulation lags about the time of entering first grade.

By contrast, the children of the socially disorganized group did not develop basically trustful object relationships in infancy. Their chaotic, impulse-driven parents frequently rejected them or related in intensely ambivalent, inconsistent ways. The children grew to be hypersensitively alert to rejection and to real and anticipated dangers in the environment. These children became "immature little drifters." Paralleling this personality disorganization were lags in language and intellectual-cognitive development.

10. Robert M. Coles, "Southern Children under Desegregation," *American Journal of Psychiatry* 120 (1963): 332-44. Coles and his co-workers longitudinally followed Negro and white children of various ages in several southern cities in the early 1960s. That both groups of children were eventually able to overcome acculturated prejudicial veneers under stressful conditions of school desegregation was attributable, Coles felt, to each group's basically sound object-relationships learned at home. Both groups of children eventually allowed themselves to respect and trust one another.

By contrast, the group of children from socially disorganized New York slum families described by Auerswald parallel in a developmental sense the lower-lower-class children described by Pavenstedt in Boston. As older children, the Auerswald group exhibited severe learning and personality disorders. They showed shallow relationships with adults and other children, very low frustration tolerance, and exhibited great difficulty in control of their impulses, both aggressive and sexual, which were discharged immediately and impulsively without delay or inhibition and often without regard to the consequences. Others had such poor relationships with formative adults that they spent considerable time in autistic reverie or exhibited interpersonal difficulty to the extent of marginal or occasional psychotic functioning.

11. Robert M. Coles, "The Lives of Migrant Farmers," *American Journal of Psychiatry* 122 (1965): 271-85.

12. Frank Riesman, Jerome Cohen, and Arthur Pearl, eds., *Mental Health of the Poor* (New York, 1964); emphasis added.

Index

Lee County, 9
literature, lack of, 16
Looff, D. H., 129, 146, 171

maladjustive trends, chronic, 37
Manchester, 155
Manchester Project, the, 9, 10, 19, 107, 112, 115, 142; clinics, 26; experience in psychotherapy, 138; field clinics, 164; health-care services, 136; home visiting, 136; success of, 131; training functions, 113-14
mental health, 24; clinics, 165; services, 136; treatment, 57
mental retardation, primary, 112
Millar, T. P., 167
Miller, Emanuel, 45, 46
ministers, talks with, 140
Mitchell, Margaret, 70
modes, infantile, 119
Morelock, Mrs., 58
motor-muscular development, 14
Muddy Gap family: case history of, 94-106; income of, 95, 104; lifestyle of, 94-96, 98; redirection of, 100-104
multiphasic screening, 20
mutism, elective, 81, 108, 109, 112; case histories, 82-84. See also "consolidated-school syndrome"

neurological deficits, 68
nonverbality, 45, 46-47, 79, 86; and conversion reactions, 69; regional, 121; relative importance with other disorders, 80; as training theme, 122
nonverbal themes, 16
nonverbal ways, 6
nurse, public health, 20, 21, 39-40, 51, 113, 114, 131, 132, 136, 165; responsibilty of, 166; as therapist, 42, 101-3

obligation, norms of, 24, 85-86
obligatory closeness, 25
OEO (Office of Economic Opportunity), 100. See also Work Experience and Training Program
O'Hara, Scarlett, 70
overprotection, 30
Owsley County, 9

parental attitudes, 26
Pavenstedt, Eleanor, 172, 173

pediatric clinic, regional, 40-41
perceptual-cognitive development, 144
personalities, effeminate, 74
personality disorders: anxious, 73, 108, 109; hysterical, 120 (see also conversion reactions); oppositional, 108, 109; overly dependent, 36, 37-38, 40, 46, 108, 109, 111, 119; overly inhibited, 108
personal-social skills, 144
physician, family, 27, 35, 41, 113, 140
physiologic symptoms, of intense anxiety, 26
"poor, hard-core," 168. See also poverty
population. See Clay County
poverty, 169. See also "cycle of poverty"; Muddy Gap family
poverty and disease, 171
"poverty syndrome, the," 170
pregnancy, false, 66
preschool development, 14
Proctor, James, 62
projective test, 47-48
psychiatric personnel, shortage of, 137
psychiatrists, 166
psychological mobility, 20
psychological treatment: crisis-oriented, 34; by public health nurses, 39
psychometric testing, 144
psychoneurotic disorders, 108, 109, 112
psychopathology: case history, 11; conflicts over sexual maturation, 112; conflicts over verbal communication, 112; regional, 118
psychophysiologic and conversion reactions, 67
psychophysiologic disorders, 8, 44-45, 176n; case histories, 44-49
psychophysiologic reactions, 25, 119
psychosexual conflict, 120, 121
psychosis, autistic. See autism, infantile
psychosomatic. See psychophysiologic
psychotherapy, 138, 139
psychotically depressed, 33
public assistance: help of, 137, 140; program, 147; workers, 113, 140
public health nurses. See nurse, public health